IMAGES
of England

THE SHEFFIELD & SOUTH
YORKSHIRE NAVIGATION

The motor barge Wharncliffe was one of the first steel craft constructed by Dunstons of Thorne. It was built as a dumb barge in 1920 for Bleasdales, who were described in records of that time as 'prime carriers interested in the Sheffield trade'. The vessel is shown discharging a cargo on the north side of Sheffield Basin in the 1960s after the company's fleet had been seized by BTW in 1958 for non-payment of tolls. The Carly float made of cork, to be used in emergencies, can be seen at the stern of the vessel, where the absence of a wheelhouse is also evident, leaving the helmsman protected from the elements by only a weatherboard. Dense cargoes such as pigs of lead and the drums shown, containing carbide, ferrochrome or ferromanganese, were off-loaded on the north side of the basin, whilst bagged materials like flour, sugar, cement and wheat would be hoisted out of a vessel moored beneath one of the straddle warehouse's five arches. Strawboard, paper reels and timber were lifted out by hand beneath the canopies on the south side of the basin and grain was discharged by bucket elevator at the silo built onto the terminal warehouse. The grille-protected berth beneath this warehouse was reserved for more valuable cargoes such as tinned foods and desiccated coconut for a local sweet manufacturer. At that time there were few cargoes loaded into craft in the basin but about 27,000 tons of cargo were handled here each year. Wharncliffe was a heavy vessel and had a draught of 6ft 4in when loaded with 90 tons of cargo. Several keels built later could carry this amount on a draught of 5ft 11in.

IMAGES
of England

THE SHEFFIELD & SOUTH YORKSHIRE NAVIGATION

Mike Taylor

TEMPUS

First published 2001
Copyright © Mike Taylor, 2001

Tempus Publishing Limited
The Mill, Brimscombe Port,
Stroud, Gloucestershire, GL5 2QG

ISBN 0 7524 2128 X

Typesetting and origination by
Tempus Publishing Limited
Printed in Great Britain by
Midway Colour Print, Wiltshire

Contents

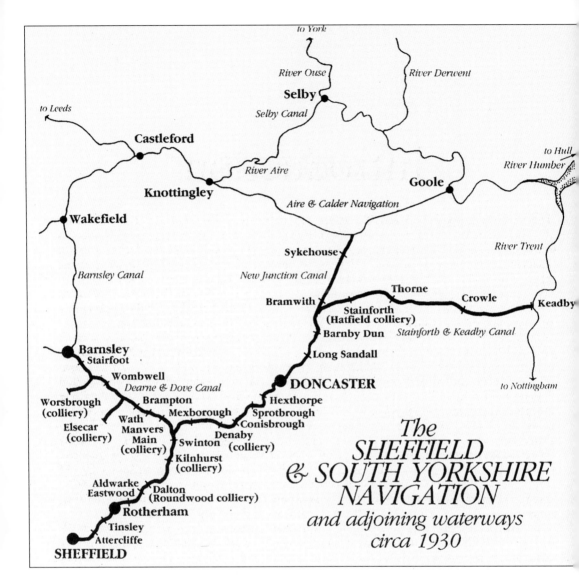

The
*SHEFFIELD
& SOUTH YORKSHIRE
NAVIGATION*
and adjoining waterways
circa 1930

Acknowledgements

For this book, I have used the Public Record Office at Kew, Sheffield Archives and standard inland waterway texts. However, my information mainly comes from the late Jim Rownsley, the late Victor Waddington, Joe Batty, Les Hill and Ken Tipton. The last three men mentioned have also been most helpful in answering my queries.

I have been allowed to dip freely into collections of photographs belonging to Alan Hall, Graham Hague, Alan Oliver, Chris Sharp of Old Barnsley and Geoff Warnes. Philip Burnitt and Christine and Graham Wilson have also given help in obtaining photographs. Laurie Thorp readily agreed to loan me his sketch of Rockingham and my own efforts with a camera have been greatly assisted by Terry Hill, Brian Webster, Bill Webster and others who welcomed me to travel aboard craft that they captained.

Introduction

The Sheffield & South Yorkshire Navigation Co. (S&SYNC) was formed in 1889 to improve the water route then existing from Sheffield through Rotherham and Doncaster to Keadby on the River Trent. Construction of a deeper waterway was envisaged, with larger locks capable of accommodating 500 ton capacity vessels and a new canal at Sheffield. This would give the wharves alongside access to the open sea whereas, hitherto, transhipment of cargoes between canal craft and sea-going vessels had usually to be undertaken at Thorne Waterside, Hull or, to a lesser extent, Goole. Neither of the latter two ports is on the S&SYN, but they belong in a complete picture of any Humber waterway and are therefore represented in this book.

Essentially, the S&SYN was based around the Don Navigation, a river navigation with canal cuts and locks for craft to bypass weirs, though in the seventeenth and early eighteenth centuries cargoes were manhandled between vessels above and below each weir. At one time, the Don's main channel fed into the River Trent but after Vermuyden's drainage work around Thorne and Hatfield in the early seventeenth century, the river flowed north to join the River Aire. Subsequently, severe flooding around Snaith and Sykehouse led to a flood channel, often called the Dutch River, being hastily cut in 1633 between New Bridge and Goole to take the Don's flow into the River Ouse. Most work on the navigation for the next 200 years concentrated on the construction or alteration of canal cuts on the Don itself. For example, before 1823 three cuts, of 473,660 and 5,600 yards, had been made to bypass sections of the old river channel and produce a continuous canal from below Doncaster to Stainforth. The other three component waterways of the S&SYN were pure canals built within twenty years of each other around 1800, with man-made channels throughout their entire lengths.

By 1845, all bridges between Keadby and Doncaster had been made to swing, adequate depth had been provided, and the first fixed-masted sea-going vessel had come to Doncaster to load coal. Shortly afterwards, in 1850, the navigation came under railway control on formation of The South Yorkshire Railway & River Dun Co. It was decided that Thorne and, later, Keadby were more suitable places at which to load coal for export so a railway was laid along the canal bank from Doncaster to deliver it to these places.

Initially, in the early 1890s, shortage of capital prevented purchase by the S&SYNC of the railway interests of the four component waterways: the River Don Navigation (navigable up to Tinsley by 1751), the Dearne & Dove Canal (1804), the Stainforth & Keadby Canal (1804) and the Sheffield Canal (1819). In 1895, however, the company began operation having had to accept railway company finances, leading to a situation where five of its ten directors were railway men. This effectively stifled competition between the waterway and the railways that almost duplicated its route.

Though the planned improved link with Keadby and the new canal at Sheffield were never constructed, despite the project resurfacing at intervals until the late 1920s, the company was ambitious. Jointly with the Aire & Calder Navigation Co. (A&CNC), it constructed the New Junction Canal linking the two navigations. This opened in 1905, improving access to Goole. It also made considerable improvements to the facilities in Sheffield Basin, most notably by building the Straddle Warehouse between 1896 and 1898. Extensive work on the locks and navigation channels at Doncaster and Sprotbrough was also undertaken before the First World War. This was done in a vain effort to make provision for the compartment boats (or 'Tom Puddings') operating on the A&CN to load at Denaby on the S&SYN (fuller details of the Tom Pudding system are given in Tempus Publishing's *The Aire and Calder Navigation* by Mike Clarke).

The S&SYN was managed efficiently and enthusiastically until the First World War when the Government took it over and gave control of food and coal deliveries to the railways. The waterway was handed back in 1920 in a badly run down condition with little maintenance work having been done for several years. There was also a shortage of craft because vessels commandeered for the war effort were never returned.

After the First World War, further work was done on straightening the channels below Doncaster but the major change was the loading of compartment boats at Hatfield colliery staithe, which began in 1933. This had been facilitated by the lengthening of Bramwith Lock the previous year. It produced a spectacular increase in the tonnage of coal carried via the New Junction Canal to Goole for tipping into sea-going vessels, which delivered it to several Thames-side gasworks and some English south-east and South Coast ports. Unfortunately, in 1934, the Dearne & Dove Canal, with its 'Manvers-size' locks, 57 $\frac{1}{2}$ft x 15ft (smaller than the 61 $\frac{1}{2}$ft x 15 $\frac{1}{2}$ft 'Sheffield-size') was closed officially as a through route between Barnsley and the S&SYN at Swinton, having been severely affected by coal mining subsidence

After over fifty years in the ownership of the S&SYNC, the waterway was nationalised in 1948 to be administered by the Docks & Inland Waterways Executive (D&IWE), a division of the British Transport Commission. The D&IWE was succeeded in 1953 by British Transport Waterways (BTW) and, in turn, they handed over to British Waterways Board (BW) in 1963. BW is still responsible for the S&SYN, though it closed its own freight depots on the navigation and ceased to carry in 1987, selling off its own craft shortly afterwards.

There were two major changes during BW's cargo-carrying days. Firstly, the Sheffield Basin was closed as the head of commercial navigation and replaced by a newly built facility at Rotherham. Secondly, there was a £16million improvement scheme between Goole and Rotherham which was completed in 1983. This finally allowed craft bigger than the 100 ton capacity Sheffield-size vessels to pass above Doncaster as far as another newly-established depot at Rotherham, through new locks with dimensions 254ft x 23ft.

Sadly, the commercial failure of the improved S&SYN has since often been given as a reason for lack of investment in other cargo-carrying waterways.

A few copies of etchings and other artworks have been included amongst the illustrations used in this book to give a glimpse of earlier days. However, photography had fortunately developed by the time the S&SYNC took over and postcards steadily increased in popularity during the early 1900s. Both of these factors have ensured that pictorial records of the navigation exist from that period. Postcards by E.L. Scrivens of Doncaster, who was active over most of the navigation from 1908 to 1939, and photographs by both Graham Hague of Sheffield and the Goole-based commercial photographer Norman Burnitt, who covered waterways between Goole and Rotherham from the mid 1950s to the late 1970s, are featured. My own photographs and those from my collection are uncredited, whilst all other illustrations are acknowledged individually. I have deliberately avoided using pictures contained in my 'Memories of the Sheffield & South Yorkshire Navigation' (1988) and 'Victor Waddington; Giant of the South Yorkshire Waterways' (1999) published by Yorkshire Waterways Publications. The illustrations in Chapter One are arranged chronologically, whilst the rest are presented topographically moving westwards from Hull towards Sheffield.

Both dry cargo and tanker barges of wooden and steel construction carrying coal, aggregate, grain, petroleum liquids and general goods appear in the book. It can be no surprise that, since over two-thirds of the navigation's annual tonnage was accounted for by coal, many of the craft shown are involved with this cargo. The vessels depicted were often built in boatyards established at various sites on the S&SYN, most often by Dunstons of Thorne. Craft are shown loading, discharging or on the move powered by horse, pull tug, push tug, sail, steam engine or diesel engine, at a wide variety of locations. These craft were operated by single boat owners as well as by the larger companies such as Bleasdales, Furleys, Harkers, Tomlinsons and Waddingtons.

One
Historical Review

Construction of locks and canal cuts enabled the Don Navigation to reach upriver as far as Rotherham by 1740. Several factories were attracted to the waterway including the glassworks shown. This was subsequently to be owned by Beatson Clarks, which was established alongside Rotherham Cut in 1751, almost ninety years before the coming of the railways. The North Midland's Leeds-Derby line was opened on land between the kilns and the canal in 1840. A gantry was then built across the railway to allow barge cargoes of coal and white sand to be discharged into the factory.

By 1751, the Don Navigation had reached Tinsley. Wharves here acted as the port for Sheffield until completion of the Sheffield Canal in 1819, construction having been delayed for decades by opposition from landowners and millers. This etching, dating from 1826, shows the canal's basin and terminal warehouse in Sheffield City Centre with the then housing-free hills beyond. Most craft working on the waterways that were eventually to become the S&SYN had a capacity of up to only 50 tons at this time. According to local newspapers which began to publish a weekly 'Sheffield Ship News', vessels arriving in the first week of the canal's life brought corn, coals, deals and groceries from Gainsborough, Doncaster and even direct from London! One vessel left for York. Trade directories of the 1820s advertised direct and regular services, without transhipment, to London, as well as to Manchester, Leeds, Liverpool, York, Gainsborough and Hull.

By the 1850s, railways had made significant inroads into waterway traffics and the four navigations eventually to become the S&SYN were under the control of the Sheffield, Manchester & Lincolnshire Railway. The Midland Railway owned the earliest Sheffield-Rotherham line and refused the MS&LR permission to construct a bridge beneath this to take the Rotherham-Mexborough line that they were constructing. Consequently, in the late 1860s, the MS&LR re-routed its waterway through Rotherham by diverting it into the river. It filled in the canal and took its railway beneath the former canal-bridge, leaving a railway bridge with towrope grooves as shown. The bridge was demolished in 1965.

Sheffield's Chamber of Commerce, casting envious eyes across the Pennines where Manchester's Ship Canal was nearing completion, wanted their own ship canal. Plans were initiated to improve their city's link with tidal waters in 1888. On this recent photograph, taken looking towards Meadowhall Shopping Centre from the motorway viaduct at Tinsley, the new ship canal was planned to leave the River Don at the bend by the central tree, with a 220ft x 30ft lock near the footbridge shown. A large terminal basin was to be built beyond two equally large locks further up the proposed waterway at Attercliffe. The actual Sheffield Canal, having risen through three locks, is just visible to the left of the photograph.

One of the first improvements made by the S&SYNC, after it began operations in 1895 with its Head Office in Sheffield Basin, was to increase warehouse space at Sheffield. A distinctive structure straddling the basin was built between 1896 and 1898: here work is shown in progress. The completed Straddle Warehouse is shown on page two.

Even before they started operating their waterway, the S&SYNC had begun, jointly with the A&CNC, to make moves towards construction of the New Junction Canal, and building began in 1896. Its main purpose was to provide access to Denaby Colliery for the latter's Tom Pudding trains, a traffic that never materialised. The 5½ mile, one lock, completely straight waterway between the A&CNC's Southfield Reservoirs and Bramwith on the S&SYN immediately provided a much easier route between the S&SYN and Goole than that afforded by the Dutch River, which joined the S&SYN at Stainforth. The construction of several aqueducts was necessary and the largest of these, comprising two 90ft spans, crossed the River Don near Bramwith. It is shown here nearing completion prior to the 1905 opening of the waterway.

Sprotbrough Bridge, Doncaster

Another improvement made in the 1900s by the S&SYN to facilitate passage of the compartment boats to Denaby was to widen the narrow channel adjacent to a water-powered corn mill in Sprotbrough Cut. It is seen here with two Doncaster-bound vessels heading down the cut towards the 1849-built stone bridge and the lock beyond. The width of the channel was increased from the 18ft shown to 38ft in 1908 and the tortuous upper junction between canal cut and river was also improved. Company minutes record that twenty-one men, one horse, one locomotive, several tip wagons, one dredger and three flats were at work on the site for several months in 1907.

In 1908, Doncaster Corporation wished to build their North Bridge over both the railway and canal to dispense with an increasingly busy level crossing. The Great Northern Railway planned to widen their bridge over the canal to carry an extra line and the S&SYN, still mindful of facilitating the movement of Puddings to Denaby, wanted to lengthen their lock to 215ft. All three projects were in close physical proximity to each other and, after numerous disputes had been settled by arbitration, work finally went ahead. This is a 1909 view looking up the navigation beneath the railway bridge. It gives a glimpse of the old canal bridge carrying the Great North Road, with a vessel in the Sheffield-size lock then extant, and the site of the new road-bridge. Work was completed in 1910.

Another Tom Pudding-fuelled alteration was made in 1932 by the lengthening of Bramwith Lock to 215ft, seen here in progress as Furleys' keel Rye, built at Selby in 1923, approaches. The work was to allow compartment boats access to Hatfield Colliery staithe and led to a very successful traffic from here to Goole, via the New Junction Canal, lasting for nearly forty years.

Opposite:
Faced with a shortage of keels on their waterway after the First World War, the S&SYN ordered seven steel sailing craft from Dunstons. These were delivered in 1925 and sold by means of Hire Purchase agreements to Furleys and Bleasdales. The venture was so successful that orders for five motor barges and six 21hp diesel engines to motorise Bleasdales' craft were placed in the mid 1930s. They were sold on under similar terms as before, the floods of 1932 having convinced the S&SYNC that motorised vessels were the craft of the future: horse-drawn keels had been held up for days whilst powered craft continued to work. Attercliffe, one of the sailing vessels sold to Bleasdales in the 1920s, is here seen loading a rare backload (of steel) in Sheffield Basin in the late 1930s, after also receiving one of the engines mentioned.

Yet another change to allow the compartment boats to reach Denaby saw construction of the last of three bypasses to cut off meanders of the old river channel below Doncaster. This one, described as the 'Doncaster Corporation North-West Development', was completed in 1934 and the aerial view shows the extent of the 'straightening' as the old channel is sealed off at its upper end leaving the gasworks on a side arm. The work was carried out by Doncaster Corporation in return for conveyance of some land and a cash payment from the S&SYNC.

1934 was also the year that the Dearne & Dove Canal was officially closed as a through route between Barnsley and the S&SYN main line at Swinton. There were two main reasons for this. Firstly, collieries feeding traffic onto the canal had become less important as deeper mines reaching thicker coal seams had been sunk further east, close to the main line of the navigation. Secondly, subsidence due to coal mining beneath the canal, estimated to be more than 10ft at some points, had reduced its draught to less than the guaranteed 4½ft. Hence the vessel shown, delivering pit props to Mitchells Main Colliery, near Wombwell, has been unable to tie up at the water's edge and lies moored in mid-channel as a distant keel is loaded at the colliery staithe. At least ten collieries on the Dearne & Dove Canal regularly loaded their coal to barges in the early 1900s, but by 1930 this had been reduced to two, though traffic continued at each end of the canal for some time after the closure. (Courtesy of the Old Barnsley Collection)

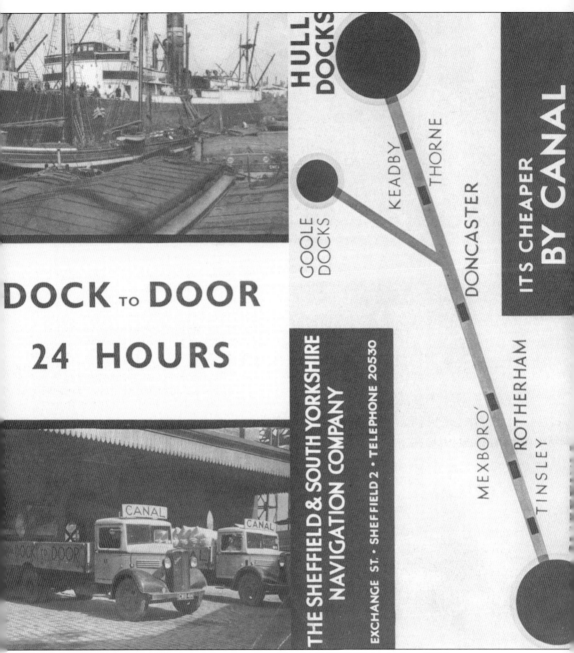

'Dock to Door', a publicity brochure produced by the S&SYNC in the late 1930s.

Upper) *Loading overside from ship to barge in Hull Docks.*

Lower) *S&SYNC's delivery and collection lorries that were based in Sheffield Basin from the mid 1930s. They worked within a 10-mile radius of the depot. The service lasted until the 1960s.*

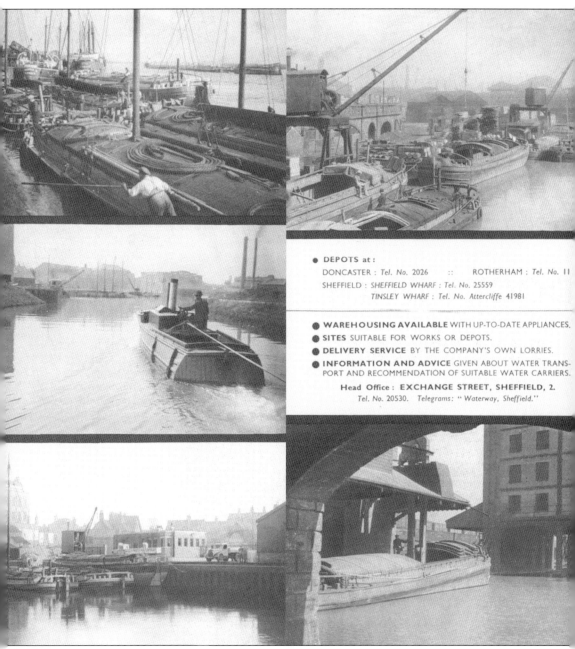

Upper) *Laden keels, having come upriver from Hull, preparing to enter the S&SYN from the River Trent at Keadby.*

Centre) *The small diesel tug* Tuna, *owned by the Keadby-based Trevethicks, which provided a towing service for keels, approaching Doncaster.*

Lower) *Craft moored at Doncaster Wharf.*

Upper) *Vessels moored at the northern wharves in Sheffield Basin.*

Lower) *A keel discharging at the grain silo and part of the straddle warehouse, viewed from the arch beneath the terminal warehouse at Sheffield.*

Until 1939, Stainforth Lock gave craft access from the canal to the Dutch River/River Don, which flowed into the Ouse at Goole and provided a route to and from the tideway, before construction of both the Stainforth & Keadby and New Junction Canals. The Goole & Sheffield Towing Company's tugs Don, subsequently replaced by Clara Marion, and Hebe towed craft on the river in the late nineteenth and early twentieth century. This service was transferred to the New Junction Canal when it opened in 1905. Don is seen hauling two craft bound for Goole downriver past Thorne Waterside having penned out of the canal at Stainforth Lock. The S&SYNC were allowed to charge tolls on the river only between Stainforth and Fishlake Old Ferry, a short distance below Thorne Waterside, and therefore had a limited interest in this waterway. Closure of the lock, which was being used by few craft at the time, forced the declining amount of traffic bound for Waterside to come upriver from Goole.

The very last improvement to the S&SYN for Denaby-bound Tom Puddings, suggested by W.H. Bartholomew of the A&CNC when the New Junction Canal was being built, related to the lengthening of Long Sandall Lock to 215ft. Here, fifty years later, in early 1959, BTW have nearly completed this work, as the motor barge Onward leaves the old lock probably heading for Hull. Though the compartment boats never reached Denaby, opening of the new lock allowed them ready access to Doncaster, and tonnages carried from here to Goole increased markedly. The trains had to be divided to pass through the lock.

Also in 1959, the private enterprise of Waddingtons of Swinton built a new wharf at Eastwood, near Rotherham on the River Don section of the navigation. Months earlier, as it was under construction, BTW in their ignorance had declared that the head of commercial navigation on the S&SYN was to be Thrybergh, two miles below Eastwood! This would have ended cargo carrying to Rotherham and Sheffield. The proposal was dropped after intervention by Sheffield City Council. Craft are shown here moored at Waddingtons' wharf in the late 1960s as a 'protest cruise' concerned with traffic to Sheffield arrives.

Initially thwarted in their efforts to move the head of navigation away from Sheffield, BTW built a new freight depot at Don Street, Rotherham in the early 1960s and this became the Head of Commercial Navigation in 1968, despite the 'protest cruise' mentioned above and several others. Thus the whole day each way taken by craft travelling between Rotherham and Sheffield to bring a cargo only a few miles nearer Sheffield was eliminated. BTW, however, claimed that the reason for the move was that Sheffield warehouses were unsuitable for the storage of the high tonnages of ferroalloys that were being imported at the time. The final cargo into the basin came in December 1970. This late 1960s picture of the new depot at Rotherham, where three craft could be handled simultaneously under cover, shows barrels of imported ferrosilicon being discharged from Lex. Staincliffe and Sobriety lie moored nearby.

The small difference between water levels above and below Conisbrough lock, after a century of mining subsidence had affected the area, led to BW opting to raise Sprotbrough Weir by 14in. This allowed the river level to increase back to Conisbrough and eliminate the difference. The lock was then demolished and here, in 1972, this work is in progress. (Courtesy of Norman Burnitt)

In 1970, BW built the push tug Freight Pioneer at Goole and the vessel is seen here after naming with two slightly smaller than Sheffield-size HS pans. Freight Trader followed the next year and both tugs worked on the ill-fated BACAT (Barge Aboard CATamaran) system which was introduced on the Humber in 1974. Pans were transferred between Hull and Rotterdam aboard a mother ship, for onward movement along inland waterways at each end of the sea voyage. On the S&SYN, pans were delivered to and collected from both Rotherham and Doncaster. However, the venture lasted only eighteen months due to fierce opposition and obstruction by Hull's dockers.

The carriage of coal at both ends of the Dearne & Dove Canal continued until beyond the Second World War, after the canal had been closed as a through route. Coal, however, was not the last cargo to be carried on the canal and here Acaster's Manvers-size Rally is delivering one of the final loads of Belgian sand from Goole to Dale Brown's glassworks at Swinton. The traffic ended in 1974. (Courtesy of Geoff Warnes)

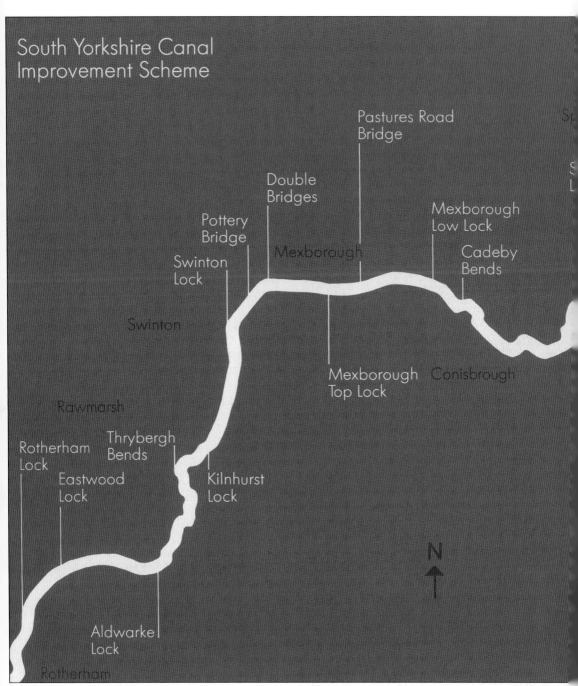

South Yorkshire Canal
Improvement Scheme

Pastures Road
Bridge

Double
Bridges

Pottery
Bridge

Mexborough
Low Lock

Swinton
Lock

Mexborough

Cadeby
Bends

Swinton

Mexborough
Top Lock

Conisbrough

Rawmarsh

Thrybergh
Bends

Rotherham
Lock

Eastwood
Lock

Kilnhurst
Lock

N

Aldwarke
Lock

Rotherham

Final details of the Improvement Scheme for the S&SYN, first proposed in 1966 at a cost of £2 million and on which work began in 1979, were given on this BW leaflet. When the Government finally gave the go ahead after years of paying lip service to inland waterways, the project cost £16million. This comprised £1million from South Yorkshire County Council, nearly £3million from a European Union development fund and a LOAN of over £12million from the British Government, which GIVES money for road construction and charges no tolls on road traffic. Huge tonnages of cargo were predicted

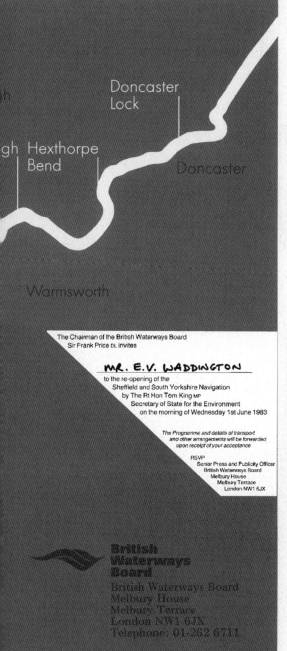

Doncaster
Lock

gh Hexthorpe
Bend

Doncaster

Warmsworth

The Scheme

The South Yorkshire Canal is one of the main commercial waterways in the north east owned and managed by the British Waterways Board. It is one of three major waterways which provide waterborne freight transport facilities between such places as Leeds (via the Aire and Calder Navigation), Nottingham (via the Trent Navigation), Rotherham and Doncaster (via the SYC) and the Humber. This direct link with the Humber Ports is the gateway to Europe and the international sea routes.

The Canal is at present used for the movement of freight in conventional barges carrying up to 500 tons to Doncaster and only 90 tons beyond there to the Rotherham/Sheffield area. Each year nearly one half of a million tons of steel, glass, wire, agricultural machinery, coal, coke, sugar and grain are carried on the waterway.

The scheme is concerned with a length of the South Yorkshire Canal between Rotherham and Bramwith, a distance of 35km, and with the New Junction Canal. Over this length, a short stretch in Rotherham consists of natural river but from Rotherham Lock to Eastwood Lock the Navigation is an artificial channel. From there the navigation follows the natural river course to Kilnhurst Flood Lock where it again enters an artificial channel, continuing through Swinton and the two locks at Mexborough to follow the natural river course again for a distance of 11km to Doncaster. It then rejoins an artifical channel through Long Sandall Lock for a further 11km where it meets with the head of the New Junction Canal at Bramwith Junction.

The scheme involves the lengthening, improvement or reconstruction of ten locks, the widening or removal of eight bridges, the major realignment of navigation channels at four sites, and the reduction of sharp curves and other present restrictions to larger craft between Doncaster and Rotherham.

The construction of swinging bays at Mexborough is necessary to allow larger craft to pass under the railway bridges. The scheme provides for the use of barges carrying up to 700 tonnes to travel as far inland as Mexborough, and those of up to 400 tonnes to reach Rotherham.

The scheme as approved will cost £10 million. The Government has applied for a grant from the European Regional Development Fund of the EEC.

for the new waterway but these never materialised. The name South Yorkshire Canal did not stick. The inset invitation to the opening of the improved waterway was sent to Waddingtons. As a General Election had become imminent, Tom King was replaced by Sir Frank Price. Mr E.V. Waddington did not attend, for he had been dead for eighteen years.

The improved navigation was opened in 1983 at a ceremony beside Eastwood Lock. High river levels and inclement weather led to curtailment of several planned activities and BW's Fair Maiden, shown here bringing VIPs upriver from Aldwarke Lock, needed assistance from the ex-Tom Pudding tug Allerton Bywater to make the voyage against a powerful current.

In 1985, the Head of Commercial Navigation was moved again, this time to a former tram and trolleybus depot in Rawmarsh Road at the upper end of the improved section, on the outskirts of Rotherham. This photograph was taken in early 2000 during one of the depot's busy periods after BW had sold it in the late 1980s. Here, Waddingtons, who eventually bought the premises and have been responsible for almost all the commercial activity on the S&SYN for the past decade, have used their fleet to carry fluorspar. This was imported via Goole to the depot and is here being transhipped to lorry for onward delivery to local steelworks.

Two
Hull and Upriver to Keadby and Goole

Until the late 1920s, many cargoes of coal were delivered from South Yorkshire collieries, usually alongside the Dearne & Dove Canal, to the steam trawlers at Hull. Here, the five-man discharge team consisting of two shovellers, two basket heavers and one basket tipper is shown in St. Andrew's Dock, Hull, transferring such a cargo from the keel in the foreground.

In the 1930s, barge captains found it more profitable to deliver coal to Hull's gasworks and cement factories than to the fish docks. Here, three coal-laden keels; Hargreaves' Eilston *and Waddingtons'* Onward *and* Victory, *lie in the Humber in the 1950s waiting to move up the River Hull with the tide, to discharge their cargoes. Sea-going vessels are also lying at anchor in Hull Roads and will lock into various docks when there is sufficient water in the river for them to do so.*

The steam keel Swiftsure *towing another vessel loaded with South Yorkshire coal up the River Hull above Drypool Bridge, accompanied by a wooden sailing keel with mast lowered and several other inland waterway craft. This, the 'Old Harbour', was the original port of Hull and attracted many industries to its banks. In 1936, the owners of* Swiftsure *were threatened with prosecution by the S&SYNC after reports that the vessel had produced a wave 2½ft high as it passed through Bramwith.*

Further up the River Hull, Branfords' Baysdale is seen in 1988 preparing to tie up below Wilmington Bridge and discharge its cargo of limestone from Cadeby, on the S&SYN near Sprotbrough,. Two tanker barges pump off their cargoes of petrol on the opposite bank. Baysdale, a former Harkers' tanker barge, has come upriver stern-first for better control on these strongly tidal waters.

The loading overside of inland waterway craft from ships took place in all Hull's general cargo docks. Here Furleys' Loxley, converted from a sailing keel four years earlier, has remained in position after transhipping a bulky cargo from Sacramento in King George Dock in 1957. (Courtesy of Associated British Ports)

Grain from Hull was a major cargo on the S&SYN. It was usually loaded via chutes at the silo in King George Dock, as shown here in the 1950s, into craft that had roughly swept out the coal delivered to the fish docks or gasworks an hour earlier. The silo was opened in 1920. Previously, grain had been loaded directly from ship to barge.

Moored at Hull's Riverside Quay, the mother ship BACAT 1 is being loaded with BACAT barges, a LASH (Lighter Aboard SHip) barge and the stern-flow unit, on its maiden visit to the port in 1974. For the first few months, five return voyages between Hull and Rotterdam were made each fortnight but, eighteen months later, this innovative operation had been halted (see page 23). In the distance, the Humber ferry Farringford may be seen heading across to New Holland.

Hanleys' Mill at Doncaster was one of those mills on the S&SYN that received supplies of grain from Hull delivered by its owners' own fleet. Initially they owned only sailing craft but, in 1937, they had the towing barge Hanleys' Pride built by Dunstons at Thorne. The vessel is seen heading up the Humber where the Humber Bridge now crosses, bound via Keadby for Doncaster. During the Second World War, with the North Sea too dangerous, wheat was imported via Liverpool and brought by train to Sheffield. Hanleys' Pride was one of several vessels that cleared each train arriving at Sheffield Basin and kept grain supplies moving in the opposite direction from usual.

A snapshot taken in 1938 from Hanleys' Pride of Hanleys' steel sailing keel Danum under tow on the River Trent bound for the company's Doncaster mill with another cargo of grain.

Three United Towing Company steam tugs in the 1930s off Keadby on the River Trent at tide time, having delivered their tows from Hull to the S&SYN entrance lock, are now assembling other craft for the return voyage. Harry Day, the Tug Broker at Keadby from 1919 until nationalisation, worked from an office on the jetty. An early morning tide time was his worst scenario as the captains of keels moored in the canal waiting for a tow to Hull had to be awakened and their vessels locked out into the Trent. They had then to be marshalled via a megaphone into positions suitable for hanging on to a particular tug bringing craft upriver. The position in the tow depended on which dock a vessel was bound for and each tug was permitted to tow a maximum of eight craft in V-formation. At the same time, Mr Day had to check that each vessel leaving the canal had two men aboard for the voyage downriver. Those captains working one-handed on the canal would have had to hire a 'purchase man'.

A tow of inland waterway craft heading down the River Trent at Keadby bound for Hull in the 1920s. They are preceded by a tow containing spritsail barges loaded with coal for English coastal ports collected from a rail-fed river staithe in the village.

Moving north to Goole on the River Ouse, another 1930s tide-time photograph shows the steam tug Goole No. 4 manoeuvring dumb craft in the river along with sea-going ships both entering and leaving the town's docks. Inland waterway craft wait to pen up out of the river. A Tom Pudding tipping hoist is visible in the docks.

An aerial view of Goole's Docks dating from the early 1930s, looking north-west. A large assembly of Tom Puddings is visible in Ouse Dock and a steam tug may be seen towing craft downriver as other vessels wait to enter the docks. Before the New Junction Canal was opened in 1905, reaching the S&SYN from Goole involved use of the fast flowing Dutch River, which may be seen entering the Ouse from the left. Even after 1905 when a wider and deeper route had been produced via Goole, keels coming from Hull to the S&SYN usually chose to voyage via Keadby because of the extra tolls required for the necessary usage of the A&CN. Not until nationalisation in 1948 were these toll discrepancies removed and, even then, the route via Keadby understandably retained its popularity with barge captains living at Thorne or Stainforth. This was despite the Goole route usually being about two hours faster.

Three a
Keadby to Bramwith

During the early nineteenth century, large quantities of coal from South Yorkshire Collieries were delivered via Keadby Lock up the Trent to Gainsborough and Lincoln. By the end of the century, however, this traffic had been attracted away to rail, though coal continued to be carried downstream for most of the twentieth century. Here, the former Furley-owned keel Balder is shown entering Keadby lock at the eastern end of the Stainforth & Keadby section of the S&SYN in the late 1960s, loaded with a cargo of gas coal bound downriver for Hull. Several craft brought coal destined for Scunthorpe steelworks by this route to Flixborough Wharf on the River Trent, but Balder's hatch covers are in place, indicating that a voyage on the occasionally rough Humber rather than a couple of miles on the Trent lies ahead. There are two pairs of gates opening in opposite directions at each end of this lock, allowing it to be used whether the water level in the tidal river is above or below that in the canal. (Courtesy of Alan Oliver)

Looking up the canal at Keadby. The Friendship public house, where horses could be stabled, lies to the left with a light keel moored beyond that has its cog boat hoisted out of the water. The cog boat, approximately 12ft long x 6ft beam, was used for many essential navigational operations off the keel as well as a lifeboat in emergencies. On the right, keels are being loaded with coal for Hull from railway wagons. It was at Keadby that the cargo on a vessel coming onto the canal had to be declared in S&SYNC days. A ticket was then issued which the captain had to have signed at toll offices passed on the voyage. Toll offices were situated at Thorne Lock, Doncaster Lock, Swinton Lock, Rotherham Depot, Tinsley and Sheffield.

Ice-breaking using a tug on the canal at Keadby in early 1940, watched by the long-serving S&SYNC Secretary and General Manager Major W.H. Pryce (in bowler hat) and Section Inspector Hanby (in trilby). The tug reportedly made little headway. The S&SYN ice-boats were damaged in this winter and two new ones were ordered shortly after the thaw came. Wooden trading craft were also especially vulnerable under these conditions, unless iron ice plates had been fitted to the bows.

Hodgsons' Richard, heading up the S&SYN in 1952 to load coal for Beverley from Hatfield Staithe, is delayed by a train crossing the waterway on a unique sliding bridge just outside Keadby. The original steam-powered swing bridge was built in 1916 as a new Keadby Bridge over the Trent was under construction. This was replaced by the electrically-operated sliding bridge shown in 1926. Both bridges were at 90° to the canal, with the railway crossing them at 45°. (Courtesy of Les Hill)

Probably the most conspicuous structure on the 13-mile long Stainforth & Keadby Canal was the Isle of Axholme Swing Bridge, which carried a railway across the waterway near Crowle. Opened in 1904 with a 100ft swinging span pivoted on a central, hollow pier standing on the towpath, the bridge was swung by a diesel engine housed in the pier. It was controlled for canal traffic by signals situated on the towpath. The bridge is shown closed looking west along the canal.

A keel with mainsail and topsail raised negotiates the Isle of Axholme Swing Bridge whilst coming up the Stainforth & Keadby Canal towards Thorne in the 1920s. These craft were often crewed by families who, unlike many narrowboat people, had a home ashore, usually at Hull, Stainforth or Thorne. The bridge was obviously built to carry a double track railway, though only a single track was ever laid. It remained in use until the line closed in 1972, when it was demolished.

The motor keel Annie H in 1983 passing Crowle station whist en route from Rampton Quarry on the River Trent to Knottingley on the A&CN in with a cargo of aggregate. The vessel was built by Dunstons in 1925 and originally rigged as a sloop.

This Scrivens postcard shows a laden keel under sail heading down the canal towards Keadby past Godnow Swing Bridge, near Crowle. These wooden swing bridges with their adjacent bridgekeepers' huts were once a feature of the Stainforth & Keadby Canal section of the S&SYN. Each bridgekeeper held out a bag as a vessel passed and it was expected that a penny would be placed in it. Pennies left at each lock encountered also added to a captain's expenses on the navigation. The railway buildings visible are, from left to right, the level crossing keeper's house, a signal box and the booking office for passengers and parcels, which stood on a very short, obscured, station platform.

A group of S&SYNC maintenance men in 1934 on the dumb workboat moored at the company's Thorne Yard waiting to be taken to Doncaster for the official opening of the new cut. The vessel was towed there by Trevethick's diesel tug Tuna. Ernie Raper (fourth from left), who gave me the photograph, claimed that the S&SYN jerseys were made especially for the occasion and replaced in their boxes after the event, never to be worn again.

Richard Dunston of Thorne became established as a chandler and ropemaker on the canal in 1858 and began building vessels at a rate of about one or two per year until 1911. Then the firm changed over completely to building craft, eventually becoming the major boatbuilder on the S&SYN. Wooden keels may be seen both under construction and being repaired in this photograph, taken in the 1910s. The company began to build steel craft in 1917 and their final new wooden vessel, the last of ninety-six, was launched in 1922.

Preparations for the launch in 1927 of the horse-drawn dumb steel tanker barge Jim are shown being made here at Dunstons' yard. The vessel had been built for Harkers, who then used it on their Keadby to Bernard Road, Sheffield, petrol traffic for over a decade. Craft were launched broadside on into the canal at Thorne, resulting in a spectacular wave flooding over the opposite bank.

Moving half a mile back down the canal towards Crowle, a bridge carrying the 1866-built Doncaster-Scunthorpe railway line is encountered. Whereas all bridges up to Doncaster had been made to swing in the 1840s, fixed bridges were allowed after the canal had effectively become owned by a railway company. This one was the first to be met when coming up from the Trent and became a great inconvenience to Dunstons as vessels designed to have even moderately tall superstructures had to be towed to the eastern side of the bridge for fitting out. This is illustrated on this 1960 photograph of the diesel trawler Grayfish. Fitting out was subsequently transferred to Hessle or Goole. As well as height restrictions on the craft built here, only those of Sheffield-size could leave up the canal via Thorne Lock. Keadby Lock limited those going down to the Trent to a 21ft beam. Even when allowed to move from the canal to the Trent without using the lock, i.e. when the water made a level, craft were limited to a length of 150ft by a bend in the canal at Thorne. Dunstons launched their last Thorne-built vessel in 1980 and left the town in 1987.

There are no locks on the drained marshland between Thorne and Keadby until the eastern end of the Stainforth & Keadby Canal, where craft transfer between the Trent and canal. A tug and three barges are here seen passing Dunstons' Yard in the 1910s as they approach the only other lock on that waterway, at Thorne. Each of the four units will have to pen up the Sheffield-size structure separately and will be lucky to move further up the canal for at least another hour.

Flixborough Shipping's Mallyan, loaded with Denaby coal bound for Scunthorpe steelworks, is shown ready to leave Thorne Lock as lockkeeper Eric Lister demonstrates his technique for opening the far side bottom gate.

Above Thorne Lock, Stanilands' Boatyard, established in the 1870s, built wooden keels until the late 1920s. Between that time, and in the 1960s, trading craft were repaired and several sailing vessels had engines installed at the yard. Honour, owned by Robinson Brothers the Rotherham millers, is shown undergoing extensive repairs, almost a rebuild, at the yard in the 1900s.

The building of a coal staithe for Hatfield Colliery in 1932 on the canal between Thorne and Stainforth led to a marked increase in tonnage figures for the S&SYN, mainly due to the coal carried by Tom Puddings, seen waiting to load on the right of this view. Other craft collected cargoes here for Doncaster and Hull and the motor barge Elma B is visible beneath the chute.

This aerial photograph, looking east, shows the village of Stainforth, home to many boating families, with the River Don/Dutch River (left) and the canal side by side. Until 1939, craft could pass between the two waterways by using a lock in the basin at the top of the photograph. There was also a small boatyard in the basin. Worfolks' Boatyard at the foot of the picture, opened in 1863, built its last vessel in 1926, and ceased trading in 1938. Until the 1930s, sailmakers and blacksmiths were established adjacent to the canal. There were also facilities near the two vessels moored beyond the bridge on the left (East) bank, where keel fitments, necessary for navigating the Humber and Trent but not needed on the canal, could be left for safe-keeping. These comprised items such as cog boats, anchors, leeboards, masts and sails. Boatmen in days of sail often filled their drinking water barrels from the spring-fed canal on this section of the waterway. The sites featured on the following three illustrations are also visible in this view.

Water sports were held annually by the canal community at several locations on Yorkshire's inland waterways. On the S&SYN, Thorne (July) and Stainforth (September) were the main locations and here the sports continued into the 1950s. Events such as walking the greasy pole and rowing a washing tub were traditional, as well as the boatwomen's sculling race illustrated here at Stainforth. The view is taken looking across the canal from a point on the left (East) bank, beyond the bridge shown on the previous picture.

A Scrivens postcard showing a horse-hauled wooden keel laden with pit props, probably imported from the Baltic via Hull, heading past Stainforth High Bridge, bound for one of the South Yorkshire Collieries. High Bridge was built in the 1850s to replace an earlier, lower swing-bridge and enable a railway line to pass through one of its abutments. It was replaced by a fixed bridge in 1948. The towpath changed sides here for the first time since the canal entrance at Keadby to pass close to the photographer. It changed over next at Bramwith Lock.

A keel with both mainsail and topsail raised is shown heading for Keadby past Stainforth's West Bank. The wide towpath shows the route of the South Yorkshire Railway and River Dun Company's 1855 single line from Doncaster to Thorne. The line was laid along the canal bank 'to obviate for the future the severe loss which the company sustains in times of scarcity of water from drought' and allow sea-going craft to load at Thorne (and later Keadby) instead of Doncaster. The railway closed after ten years of use, having been partially by-passed and replaced by a more direct double-track line from Doncaster to Keadby and Scunthorpe.

The diesel Tom Pudding tug West Riding, built by Dunstons in 1958, and empty compartments are shown on the S&SYN at Bramwith, bound for Hatfield Staithe to load coal for Goole. The 'jebus' being pushed fits in front of the train of pans after loading to deflect the tug's wash. The units are held together by chains with a stempost projecting from each compartment sitting in a corresponding groove on the stern of the one in front. (Courtesy of Norman Burnitt)

Three b
Goole to Bramwith

(i) Via the Dutch River

Half a mile above the confluence of the Dutch River and River Ouse at Goole there is a swing bridge carrying a road over the former. At 'Dutch River Wharf' on the south side of the river above this bridge, the ex-Harker tanker barge Ribblesdale H *is seen, at low water, discharging a dry cargo to lorry in the 1980s.*

In early 2000, Waddingtons' tug Strongbow *(formerly the Tom Pudding tug* Allerton Bywater*) is seen heading down the Dutch River towards the swing bridge pushing the company's No 40, loaded at the wharf shown above with imported fluorspar for Rotherham. (Courtesy of Mike Brown)*

G.D.Holmes's motor barge Quit *broke loose from its moorings at Goole's Dutch River Wharf in early 1958 and drifted downstream, eventually holing itself on the swing bridge and ruining its cargo of potash. Here, the company's David Sugden and former Harker tug* Lion *are attempting to salvage the stricken vessel. At least* Quit *did not jam the bridge against road users, as several coasters have done to the great inconvenience of residents of Old Goole. (Courtesy of Norman Burnitt)*

Since the Second World War, few craft have ventured onto the tidal Dutch River above the wharf at Goole. Here, however, Alan Oliver's ex-BW workboat Grampus *is seen heading upriver above Rawcliffe Bridge in 1996, bound for New Bridge where it was due to take away used sandblast. The disused chimney lies alongside the A&CN.*

The only major site of activity on the Dutch River away from Goole was at Thorne Waterside, a prosperous village before the Stainforth & Keadby Canal was opened in 1804. Traffic almost ended after Stainforth Lock was closed in 1939 but Chambers kept their crushing mills open and here Pattrick's sailing keel Medina *is seen preparing to head downriver after discharging a cargo of imported locust beans at their wharf in 1940. The late Mrs Evelyn Holt, who was mate with her father on the vessel for eighteen years, gave me the photograph.*

Thorne Waterside was both a port and a boatbuilding centre before construction of the Stainforth & Keadby Canal. From 1750 for half a century it was the primary cargo transhipment point between sea-going and inland waterway craft on the navigation. Steam packets provided a regular passenger and goods service to Hull during the first half of the nineteenth century. One of the paddle steamers used was Rockingham, which was probably built here and is shown in this sketch by Laurie Thorp, based on a painting by Thomas Binks. The river was rerouted away from Waterside during the 1950s as part of flood prevention work and the village's only claim to present day fame is as the birthplace of the singer Lesley Garrett.

(ii) Via the A&CN and New Junction Canal.

The Port of Goole opened in 1826 and this postcard, used in 1910, shows steam-powered and sailing ships as well as inland waterway craft in Barge Dock, one of the original docks. Extensive ship/barge transhipment of cargoes has always taken place at Goole and continues to this day, though at a much reduced level.

One of numerous 'trial loads' that came down the S&SYN after its 1983 improvement is shown here. Holgates' Anne M Rishworth with the dumb barge Pat lashed alongside crosses Goole's West Dock loaded with steel from Rotherham for export in the Russian ship on the left of the photograph. Another motor/dumb barge pair is following with a further part of the consignment.

Compartment boat trains loaded at canalside collieries converged on Goole from the 1860s to the 1980s and, until the 1950s, were handled by steam-powered tugs. The one shown here is hauling a small train of pans to one of the hydraulically operated tipping hoists in the docks. Strangely, after nationalisation, responsibility for tipping pans was vested with the port authorities, whilst their movement to and from the collieries was left in the hands of the waterway body – a situation which created a few problems!

Beyond the assembly of coal-filled compartments, the ship Henfield is shown on this postcard being loaded from the tipping hoist in Ouse Dock during the 1950s. The coal was delivered to English and nearby European destinations.

The Tom Pudding system ended its days with diesel tugs pulling pans loaded at Doncaster on the S&SYN with smokeless fuel, the final run being in 1986. The ship Kando is here being loaded with such a cargo for Scandinavia in 1985 at the hoist in Goole's South Dock, as one of the diesel tugs brings more loaded pans to the hoist.

Looking from the top of a dockside mill into Barge Dock and over to the River Ouse in the 1950s, Bleasdales' Dovecliffe and Eastcliffe are shown, lashed together, heading westwards towards the A&CN. (Courtesy of Norman Burnitt)

The push tug Freight Trader *in BW's dry dock at Goole with its two 360° rotatable Schottel propulsion units under repair. This became a common occurrence due to impact with the riverbed whenever the tug pushed its 170ft long three-barge assembly on the twisting river sections of the S&SYN.*

Stainforth, *one of the powered craft built by Dunstons in 1936 to be sold by the S&SYNC under Hire Purchase to a barge operator, is seen at Camplings' Yard, Goole. The photograph was taken in 1966 as the vessel was being lengthened by insertion of a new mid-section to increase its carrying capacity.*

Another 'trial load' for the improved S&SYN being delivered to Goole for export. This time it is Acasters' Easedale H approaching the port along the A&CN with a cargo of pitch from Kilnhurst. Unfortunately this happened during the miners' strike of 1984 when pickets delayed the vessel because they believed it was carrying coal. The ship left without this load which then melted over the subsequent hot weekend and could not be discharged after it had solidified on cooling. The vessel returned to Kilnhurst with its cargo, which was eventually unloaded.

In the 1920s, various craft, crudely adapted by dropping tanks into them and with few safety precautions in place, delivered petrol along the S&SYN to Rotherham and Sheffield. Two Sisters, a barge thus converted, exploded at Keadby with loss of life in 1926. This photograph shows an incident at New Bridge on the A&CN in 1929 as the horse-drawn petrol barge Whitaker's No 16 caught fire and exploded whilst en route for Rotherham. The barge captain was blown into the canal and eventually persuaded by an AA patrolman to allow himself to be taken to Doncaster Infirmary. He subsequently made a full recovery, though the vessel's 18,000 gallon cargo blazed for fourteen hours. In 1936, Jim, a purpose-built tanker, was also involved in an incident. Whilst passing through Thorne 'flames 50ft high' were produced when a passer-by discarded his cigarette into the canal shortly after the vessel's bilges had been pumped out. To the captain's enormous relief, application of a fire extinguisher put out the flames as they advanced towards Jim's cargo.

John Dean's Jolly Miner, *loaded with limestone from Cadeby, bound, via Goole, for a wharf on the River Hull (see page 29), leaving the New Junction Canal for the A&CN at Southfield Reservoirs in 1990.*

The usual seventeen pan Tom Pudding tow to and from Doncaster had to be split to pass through locks at both Sykehouse and Long Sandall, even after lengthening of the latter. Here, in 1981, tugmaster George Parkinson walks along his diesel tug Brodsworth *as the tug, jebus and seven pans are lowered in the New Junction Canal's Sykehouse Lock. The remaining ten loaded pans wait above the lock to be penned down afterwards, before being reconnected to the front section of the train and taken to Goole. The four-man crews slept aboard the tugs until the 1960s but, by the time this picture was taken, they managed to travel from Goole and back within a day.*

BW used the old steam Tom Pudding tugs, made redundant by new diesel tugs, in ice breaking on the New Junction Canal during the 1960s. The purer water here, as at Stainforth Ings, was often used to fill a boatman's drinking water barrel in the days of sail. In a cold spell, it always froze first; here, the tug Whitwood *has been beaten by the ice as it attempts to keep the motor barge* Hatfield *moving early in 1963.*

Waddingtons' Sheffield-size motor barge Heritage, *also built by the Swinton company, crossing the New Junction Canal's Don Aqueduct in 1997 loaded with fluorspar for Rotherham. The guillotine gates at each end were added during the Second World War. When lowered in times of flood, they prevent excess water entering the canal from the river.*

Four
Bramwith to Doncaster

Just above the junction of the New Junction Canal and the S&SYN main line near Bramwith, lay the coal-fired Thorpe Marsh Power Station. During its lifetime, it received only few cargoes by water and these were of fuel oil in the late 1980s and early 1990s. Whitakers' Fusedale H is shown arriving with such a cargo loaded at Immingham whilst their Humber Enterprise is turning to return for another load after pumping off. The final cargo of oil was delivered here in March 1994.

Flixborough Shipping's Sheffield-size Littlebeck *is shown leaving the new 215ft long lock at Long Sandall in 1969 loaded with Denaby coal bound via Keadby for Scunthorpe steelworks. BW's dredging plant lies moored to the left on the approach to the old lock.* (Courtesy of Norman Burnitt)

Some of the owners of pleasure boats began using the old lock at Long Sandall as an improvised dry dock. With the lock full, a vessel was tied firmly to the bollards on each side of the lock, which was then emptied, leaving the boat suspended from its ropes and able to be painted or otherwise maintained. The practice was ended when BTW removed the bottom gates of this lock rendering it impossible to fill. This is the situation in this 1962 aerial view of the locks, three years after construction of the new long lock. (Courtesy of the Bob Pearce Collection)

The S&SYN has never been as attractive to pleasure craft as the narrow canals of the Midlands, perhaps because leisure users were likely to encounter large working craft on the move at the peak of canal cruising's popularity. Nevertheless, Strawberry Island Boat Club was established in 1969 on one of the meanders characteristic of the old course of the Don below Doncaster that had been by-passed in 1902. This aerial view, from 1,500ft looking west, shows club members' craft moored on the old river course; the lock cut with the present navigation channel and the river flood-relief course are visible at the top of the picture. The actual 'island' lay between the river and lock cut which were bypassed: it is barely visible at the foot of the photograph. (Courtesy of the Dave Smith Collection)

Active well before the 'Doncaster Corporation North-West Development' of 1934, local photographer Matthew Henry Stiles produced some excellent waterway shots. Here, the laden wooden sailing keel Surprise of Beverley is shown on one of his views heading down the navigation towards the gasworks, well before the stretch of water being used was by-passed in the development (see page 16).

A photograph taken in 1934 as the new channel bypassing the gasworks neared completion. A sailing keel is seen heading down the navigation along the old channel.

After 1934, the old channel was sealed off at its upper end, leaving an arm to the gasworks lower down the navigation at the other end of the new channel. Here, the arm is in use during 1982 after the gasworks had ceased to use coal, as improvement works were taking place further up the navigation. Waddingtons' Confidence *pushed by their* Kingfisher *had* delivered the first of four large 333 ton German castings from Goole. This was being lifted out of the vessel for an extremely difficult onward movement to Sheffield by road.

The steam tug Hebe passing Brooke's Wharf as it arrives in Doncaster with a train of barges. The photograph was featured in an advertisement published in the early 1900s for the Goole and Sheffield Transport Co., which subsequently became W. Bleasdale & Co.. The tug and barges would have used the Dutch River to come from Goole since the New Junction Canal would not have been opened at the time.

With Brooke's Wharf visible beyond, Hanleys' Mill at Doncaster, the destination of much waterway grain traffic from Hull since the mid-nineteenth century, is shown in the distance along with two keels ready to sail down the navigation. The view was taken in the 1900s after the large fire of 1881 at the mill but before a second fire in 1923, which caused it to close until 1925. The rebuilt mill resumed its supplies of grain by water but was demolished in the 1970s.

Smokeless fuel is shown being tipped down the chute at Doncaster, just above Hanleys' (then Ranks') Mill, from a lorry that had brought it from Wingerworth, near Chesterfield, into a Tom Pudding in the late 1970s. The cargo would be transferred again when it reached Goole on its way to Scandinavia.

A slick changeover in the early 1980s as the jebus brought from Goole at the front of an empty Tom Pudding train is cast off at Doncaster to be fastened to the train of loaded pans that are ready for the return journey.

The most popular vantage point for postcard photographs of the S&SYN in the early twentieth century has been used for this Scrivens view of keels moored at Doncaster with St. George's Church in the background.

Doncaster's first electric power station was built in Greyfriars Road below the railway bridge during 1899 for its public transport service. Motor vessels including Michael H are seen moored alongside in the late 1940s prior to or after delivering coal from S&SYN colliery loading staithes. A new power station opened above the lock in the early 1950s and the premises shown were retained as a back-up facility for a short time afterwards.

Hubert Barrass's ex-Furleys' motor vessel Lys entering Doncaster lock in the 1970s bound for Rotherham with grain from Hull. (Courtesy of P.L. Smith)

In 1960 BTW built a wharf immediately above Doncaster Lock and used it mainly to tranship cargoes brought from Hull by larger vessels such as Tees, shown here in 1963, into smaller vessels able to pass through the locks above Doncaster and reach Rotherham and Sheffield. In the mid-1970s, BACAT cargoes were also handled here. (Courtesy of Geoff Warnes)

The top and intermediate gates of Doncaster lock are shown almost underwater during the floods of 1932 on this postcard view with traffic halted. It was situations such as this that convinced the S&SYN management that motor keels were superior to horse-drawn vessels as the latter remained tied up for many more days with the towpath submerged. The canal cut lying straight ahead was opened in 1843. Prior to this, craft followed the river round to Mill Bridge, at the end of Marshgate, and locked through there.

Doncaster's second power station opened in 1954 on Campsall Fields which can be seen, waterlogged, in the distance on the right of the previous illustration. Waddingtons' vessels are shown in 1975 delivering coal from Denaby to the adjacent basin, built on the course of the River Cheswold. The station closed in 1981 and was demolished shortly afterwards to make way for 'Doncatraz', a prison surrounded by high walls. (Courtesy of Les Reid)

Five

Doncaster to Sprotbrough

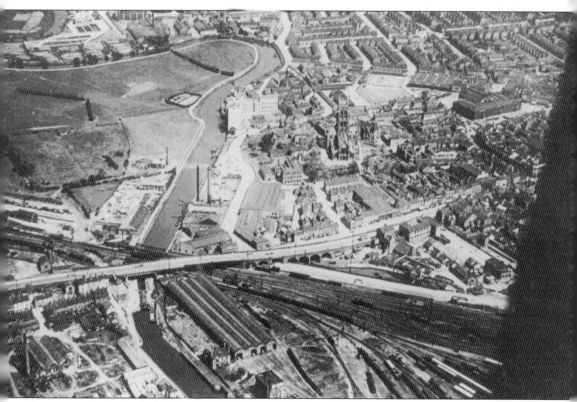

This 1930s aerial view looking down the navigation from above Campsall Fields at Doncaster, well before construction there of the power station, shows most of the sites featured in the latter part of the previous chapter. These include the gasworks, the site of Doncaster Corporation's North-West Development, Hanleys' Mill, the old power station, the railway bridge, North Bridge and Doncaster Lock. From this point, for 10½ miles upstream to Tinsley, the S&SYN was and still is a river navigation with lock cuts to bypass weirs.

A keel sailing down the River Don at Hexthorpe near the site of a petrol depot that was water-served until 1964 is featured on this photograph by Matthew Henry Stiles dating from the 1920s.

NEW RAILWAY BRIDGE
6   HEXTHORPE FLATTS

The 'new' bridge on the printed caption to this postcard picture refers to the four-span lattice girder crossing built in 1910 to carry the Great Central Railway's double track 'Doncaster-avoiding line' across the River Don. The wooden keel Chance is sailing downriver towards Doncaster. The S&SYNC ensured that the bridge would be built with sufficient headroom that a vessel's mast and sails would not usually have to be lowered to pass beneath it. Limestone from Levitt Hagg will have been used to surface the well-maintained towpath on the left. The bridge is still in use.

Waddingtons' former tanker barge Lonsdale, *built in 1947 by Harkers of Knottingley, approaching the A1(M) viaduct at Sprotbrough as it heads upriver in July 2000 with a cargo of Lithuanian steel bound for Rotherham. Before conversion to a dry cargo barge and lengthening, this vessel was involved in petrol deliveries to Hexthorpe.*

Onward *pushing* Heritage *down the River Don below Sprotbrough in 1978. Both vessels were owned by Waddingtons and each one was loaded with 100 tons of coal from Denaby for Doncaster Power Station.*

A sailing keel entering Sprotbrough Lock in the 1900s. The mast and sails would be left at Mexborough for safe keeping and a horse hired to take the vessel further up the navigation where numerous bridges made sailing impracticable.

One of the practical difficulties in handling BACAT trains was their passage above Doncaster. A three-barge tow took four pennings at each Sheffield size lock with the barges usually handled by 'human horses' as shown here at Sprotbrough. This made what was a smooth and efficient service over on the Rhine and below Doncaster into a very time-consuming exercise between Doncaster and Rotherham.

An inspection of the S&SYN in 1946 with the company's 'bus boat' below the bridge in Sprotbrough Cut. The boat was constructed by fitting an engine into a dumb maintenance vessel and lowering an old Rotherham Corporation bus body into it. It was used as a VIP/inspection boat from 1946 until the early 1950s.

A keel starting to lower its sail to pass beneath the photographer's vantage point on Sprotbrough Bridge as it heads towards Doncaster in the 1920s after the channel by the mill had been widened to 38ft (see page 13) in 1908.

Taken from the same viewpoint after the waterway had been widened much more in the improvements of the early 1980s, Acaster Water Transport's push tug Little Shifta and two loaded lighters head for Rotherham. Built by Dunstons in 1953 as the pull-tug Snatchette for work on the River Medway, the vessel returned to the Humber Waterways in 1983 when it was converted to a push tug and a retractable wheelhouse was fitted.

Six
Sprotbrough to Denaby

Before the smooth and wide present day merging of the River Don and the top end of Sprotbrough Cut, the cut bent round to form a T-junction with the river close to the weir over which several craft have been swept in flood conditions. Here, a keel heading downriver in the 1900s has just entered the cut from the river and lowered its sail. The entrance was smoothed out in the 1908 improvements and several times since then, attaining its present shape and width during the improvements of the early 1980s.

Sprotbrough Weir was raised in 1972 and work on this task by BW men and machinery is shown in progress (see page 22). (Courtesy of Norman Burnitt)

A view of Sprotbrough Weir and Cut from a hot-air balloon in the 1990s with Waddingtons' Confidence, bound light for Goole, being pulled down the navigation by the tug Kingfisher. The steel girder bridge across the canal was built in 1933 at Denaby and Cadeby Collieries' expense after the stone bridge (shown on page 13) had been rendered unsafe due to subsidence caused by coal workings. (Courtesy of Alan Oliver)

L.S. 60-4. Levitt Hagg.

Levitt Hagg, on the Don's right bank, was a quarrying and lime-burning village from the eighteenth century until evacuated on hygiene grounds shortly after the Second World War, because the polluted River Don tended to contaminate drinking water whenever it flooded. Until the railway was built in the mid-nineteenth century, coal for the kilns was brought by barge from local collieries and both limestone and quicklime were carried away by water, much of these going via the Dearne & Dove Canal to glassworks in the Barnsley area. This Scrivens postcard uses a photograph from the 1890s and shows the boatbuilding that also took place in the village. The final vessel to be built here is shown in the early days of construction and was launched in 1899 as Dorothie. A clinker-built (overlapping planks) keel is moored nearby. This method of constructing wooden craft was superseded by carvel building (abutting planks) early in the twentieth century.

Lime and limestone chutes can just be seen as a keel sails down the River Don past Levitt Hagg and its quarries in the 1900s. This stretch of the S&SYN was bridge-free and ideal for sailing if there was a fair wind. The rowing boat was probably hired from Conisbrough. (Courtesy of the Alan Oliver Collection)

Viewed from the railway viaduct in 1989, John Dean's Bonby is seen loading limestone for Hull at Cadeby Quarry. The dumper truck used is on the loading staithe built in 1985 by Alan Oliver Workboats.

BW's Maureen Eva *featured strongly in Tempus Publishing's 'The River Trent Navigation' and, as trade on the Trent declined, the self-propelled vessel made several voyages on the improved S&SYN. In 1988, after BW had ceased commercial work with their own craft, Maureen Eva was sold to Alan Oliver who used it to carry, amongst other cargoes, limestone for Hull loaded at the staithe he built at Cadeby. Unfortunately, whilst being loaded, a clumsy mechanical shovel operator tipped too much limestone into the vessel which is shown shortly afterwards sitting on the river bed as efforts were being made to raise it. The barge operated successfully after being refloated and is still available for work.* (Courtesy of Sheila Bury)

A postcard view of Rainbow Bridge, admired for its 'splendid cast iron arch of three huge ribs with beautiful spandrels', which took the 1849-built railway over the River Don at Cadeby. The 600 tons of iron used was cast at nearby Conisbrough. A sailing keel may be seen heading downriver. As both trains and locomotives became heavier, the bridge was replaced by a sturdier, but much less attractive, structure in 1928.

The bridge built to replace Rainbow Bridge is shown here in Summer 2000 from a similar viewpoint. Alan Oliver's Wyre Lady passes beneath it on a 'waterbus' service over what is generally considered to be one of the most attractive stretches of the entire S&SYN. Wyre Lady was the former Clyde ferry Ashton, built at Dumbarton in 1938, and acquiring its present name in the early 1970s after becoming Fleetwood's Knott End ferry across the River Wyre. After a brief period on the River Severn, the vessel was brought to the S&SYN in 1978 and, based at Sprotbrough, has carried private parties and general passengers on the waterway ever since.

The 528-yard Dearne Valley Railway Viaduct at Conisbrough was built between 1907 and 1908 and was undoubtedly the greatest engineering undertaking ever witnessed in the Doncaster area. Great use was made of a 3 ton capacity overhead cableway stretching across the valley during construction. On this downstream view, the 130 ton span over the river had yet to be built and eased across from the right bank, 115ft above the river. There are fourteen arches on the Cadeby (left) bank and seven on the Conisbrough side. A one-coach passenger train service crossed on the single line until 1951 and coal trains continued after this. The viaduct still stands.

A view of Conisbrough Viaduct, looking downstream, from a coal barge bound for Doncaster Power Station in the 1970s.

BW's press release described a '500 ton tanker' bringing 'oil products' to Kilnhurst on what was hoped would become a 10,000ton per year traffic and this delivery, featuring one of the first larger-than-Sheffield size vessels to come this far upriver, received considerable publicity. In reality, Whitakers' ex-Harker tanker Fossdale, seen here heading upriver in 1983 from the top of Conisbrough Viaduct, was carrying only about 350 tons of tar due to the poor standard of the improvement works at Hexthorpe. A further 2,000 tons of this cargo came up the S&SYN during the next few months. There was then a period when little seemed to happen until, amazingly, the entire cargo was brought back downriver, unused and untreated, by the same craft that had taken it up a couple of years earlier. (Courtesy of BW)

The steam-powered bucket dredger No.4 was purchased by the S&SYNC in 1924 and is shown on this newspaper cutting at work near Conisbrough in the 1940s, before nationalisation. The Don in flood deposited bars of silt across cut ends as it raced past them, making efficient dredging essential to maintain the guaranteed depth of water. The dredger pulled itself methodically over the river bed using chains fastened to each bank and discharged the sludge brought up by the continuous chain of buckets via a chute into 25 ton capacity pans moored alongside. Up to 200 tons of dredgings were taken to Sprotbrough each day in the horse-drawn pans and deposited on the banks. Until the 1970s, dredgers worked almost daily on the navigation, new diesel-powered craft being purchased for the purpose in the 1950s. Shortly after the 1983 improvements, however, these were replaced by much less efficient boat-mounted motor grabs capable of making only random 'bites' at the accumulated silt. This gave substance to the late Victor Waddington's accusation that BW concentrated their efforts on the above-water appearance of the S&SYN whilst ignoring the state of affairs below the water.

Conisbrough Lock and Lockhouse are visible to the right of this 1910s upstream view of the river and lock cut. A keel discharging its cargo of Swedish birch for the nearby woodturner's premises is visible above the weir where a waterwheel provided him with the necessary power. Conisbrough Castle, the setting for Athelstane in Sir Walter Scott's Ivanhoe, may be seen beyond this.

A turn of the century view of Conisbrough Lock from above. The river went off to the right to pass over a weir and craft rejoined it after a very short lock cut. In times of high river levels, many captains avoided using the lock when travelling downriver and saved time by coming straight over the weir.

Waddingtons' Progress, formerly Harkers' tanker Ennerdale H pushing their dumb barge Vivos beneath Conisbrough Railway Bridge, which carries the Doncaster-Sheffield line at Conisbrough. The photograph was taken in 1999 as the craft were bound for Rotherham with fluorspar.

A view from Cadeby Colliery of the Don with Denaby in the distance as a motor vessel heads downriver. There were three railway bridges across this stretch of the river between Mexborough Low Lock and Conisbrough Lock. Sailing craft coming downriver would often be hauled from the bank with mast and sail lowered using a 'man's line' and canvas 'seal' hooped around the mate's chest. The captain meanwhile would be handling the tiller and occasionally giving assistance by wielding the 'stower'. The Earth Centre, one of several currently financially failing Lottery-funded ventures in South Yorkshire, has since been built on the colliery site.

Denaby Colliery Staithe was one of the busiest on the S&SYN from the time it opened in 1863 until it closed in 1981. Railway wagons both from this colliery and later from Cadeby Colliery, which opened in 1893, were brought to the staithe and tipped as shown into waiting inland waterway craft. The wooden keel Zelda is shown loading here for Flixborough in 1960 after an engine had been fitted into the originally dumb vessel.

Joe Batty, a boatman who has probably worked on the S&SYN for more hours than anyone else, preparing to moor Waddingtons' Northcliffe at Denaby staithe in 1977. The helmsman's exposed position is clearly shown with only the folded-down weatherboard for protection from the elements. An iron canal tiller dating from dumb boat days is being used; this allowed the rudder to be put hard over, thus giving greater manoeuvrability than the bulkier wooden variety which had more leverage and was kept for use on tidal rivers. Most sailing craft had both types but after being motorised they usually retained only the wooden one. Spoil heaps from Cadeby Colliery are visible in the background. These have subsequently been 'landscaped'.

If vessels carried on straight ahead at the bend, instead of following the river round to Denaby Staithe, they would come to Mexborough Low Lock as Danum has done here on its voyage from Hull. The vessel, seen on page 31 as a sailing keel, has since been motorised and also passed to Ranks' ownership like the mills at both Rotherham, to where it is heading, and Doncaster. The bridge over which coal wagons were brought from Cadeby Colliery to the staithe and more spoil heaps lie beyond the vessel. In 1913, the S&SYNC recorded that this lock had bodily subsided 3ft due to the nearby colliery workings.

Seven
Denaby to Swinton

Moving about one mile up the almost featureless 1844-built cut between Denaby and Mexborough, these two 1954-built coal loading staithes were designed to be used for three or four years, whilst local roads were being improved. They were constructed to transfer coal brought from nearby collieries by lorry into ex-Leeds & Liverpool Canal craft, for delivery to the new power station at Doncaster. BTW's strange policy of paying their men to travel from and back to Leeds each day in their 'working hours' caused shortages at the power station. After initially helping out, Waddingtons eventually took over deliveries and loading was then transferred to Denaby. A snow-covered Cadeby Colliery spoil heap can be seen in the distance.

Mexborough's Pasture Bridge is next to be met along the cut. Here, towing horses crossed over the canal as the towpath changed sides. BTW's maintenance boat Endurance *is being used in 1956 on re-piling work and widening of the canal in connection with construction of a new road bridge. The canal is almost drained and extensions to the nearby power station are approaching completion. In pre-nationalisation days,* Endurance *was also used at regular intervals to deliver the coal allowance given to S&SYN lockkeepers from Denaby Staithe. The power station was demolished in 1988 having never received a single cargo of coal by water.*

Entering Mexborough, Bull Green Boatyard, one of three in the town, was encountered. Constructed in 1899 by two members of the Waddington family, it was in use for only about ten years. The wooden keel moored at the yard had just been named Comity (defined as courtesy, mildness and kindness). It was built in 1909 for William Pattrick and, until sold on in 1934, worked regularly from Hull, up the Dutch River to Thorne Waterside. After discharge of its cargo of seeds for crushing, the vessel usually sailed light to Stainforth Lock and joined the S&SYN main line to come to Denaby for a load of coal to take back to Hull. The vessel subsequently returned to Waddingtons who used it on their coal traffic between Rotherham and Blackburn Meadows Power Station during the Second World War.

This postcard view looking down the navigation shows a clinker-built keel moored by Woffindins' masting yard below Mexborough Top Lock in the 1910s. As sailing craft came up the S&SYN, equipment not needed on the canal was dropped off for safe keeping at various points and collected on the return voyage. Leeboards were often left at Thorne or Stainforth and cog boats and anchors at Thorne, Stainforth, Bramwith or Long Sandall. Here at Mexborough, or at Stainforth, masts and sails were lifted off by hand-cranes onto trestles, leaving the vessels to navigate the locks and bridgeholes towards Sheffield hauled by a horse hired for the purpose.

Mexborough-based Horse Marine John Ward and his horse posing for the camera above Mexborough Top Lock in 1910 prior to towing a vessel waiting in the lock up the navigation. Horse haulage on the S&SYN lasted until the Second World War. There used to be horse marines for hire at Doncaster as well as at Mexborough but, by 1937, company records indicate that these had dwindled to nine at Mexborough and one at Doncaster. Charges for the services of a horse and marine were calculated by dividing the Sheffield-Keadby run into five different five or six hour stages between Keadby, Thorne, Doncaster, Mexborough, Rotherham and Sheffield. A marine was booked by telegram or by telephoning a lock near his base. The boat captain was responsible for the marine's food and usually allowed him to sleep on the cabin lockers. There were stables at several pubs near the navigation and the S&SYNC also provided them at some of the locks.

1. The Ferry, Mexborough.   Copyright.   Scrive

In 1834, the Kilnhurst-Mexborough Canal Cut was extended slightly and the lock by which craft passed between this and the River Don was moved a short distance east from Mexborough Church, near to the present site of Mexborough Top Lock. In 1844, the canal cut was extended by over a mile to Denaby, terminating in Denaby (or Mexborough Low) Lock linking canal cut and river. On the river section thus bypassed lay the centuries-old ferry between Mexborough and Old Denaby for which the Don Navigation Company had assumed responsibility. This passed to the S&SYNC who provided both the ferryman and the boat used. On this Scrivens postcard, the ferryboat is preparing to cross to Mexborough above the weir that ensured a sufficient depth of water for it.

In 1964 the ferry was replaced by a bridge and another was built to replace the swing bridge over the canal above Mexborough Top Lock. Waddingtons' Victory was hired to help with the latter and is shown moored close to the construction site. (Courtesy of Geoff Warnes)

Glass manufacture and blowing was one of Mexborough's major industries for several decades around 1900. One of the biggest bottle manufacturers were Barrons, who had premises alongside the canal and used it extensively for the import of raw materials and export of finished goods, claiming that breakages by water transport were minimal. Here, coal is seen being craned off a keel moored at the company's wharf on the town side of the canal in 1910.

The canal was rerouted to make a right-angled left turn as it approached Swinton when the railways came to Mexborough in the mid-nineteenth century. Branfords' Cordale is shown negotiating this bend to pass beneath Double Bridges (both railway bridges) as it heads for Rotherham in 1986. Considerable work was necessary here to accommodate large craft as the improvements of the early 1980s were being made. The bridge nearest the camera carried the Doncaster-Barnsley line opened in 1849.

In this photograph, taken in 1956 from Swinton's Pottery Bridge, with water levels lowered, a wooden maintenance flat is being poled and bow hauled up the navigation, past the old MS&LR station towards Swinton Lock. A distant vessel may be seen moored outside Swinton Gasworks, though at this time piped coal gas was being received direct from Manvers' Main Coking Plant. The final usage of horses to haul craft on the S&SYN took place in 1947 when the navigation company used the type of vessel shown to resurface towpaths with limestone loaded at Levitt Hagg.

A BW maintenance boat is seen leaving the manually-operated Sheffield-size lock at Swinton in the late 1970s before a large, new mechanised lock was built here. In the 1840s, before the Doncaster-Barnsley railway had been built, a traveller wishing to go from Rotherham or Sheffield to Hull would come to Swinton by rail on the Derby-Leeds line. He would walk down to the canal at this point to catch the aquabus, which would be horse-hauled at speed down the navigation to Doncaster. Here, a horse-drawn coach would be picked up to reach Thorne and either a paddle steamer boarded at Waterside to make the final stage of the journey, or another aquabus used to reach Keadby by canal where the Gainsborough-Hull Packet could be caught. (Courtesy of BW)

Eight
Swinton to Barnsley

A boatyard on the Dearne & Dove Canal, two locks up from its junction with the S&SYN main line, was established in the nineteenth century. From 1923 until the present time, it has been the base of Waddingtons' canal carrying, boat maintenance and woodyard operations. Few craft were actually built by them at the yard. However, steel shells constructed elsewhere for the company were completed here, having their cabins furnished, hatch covers constructed and engines installed. Onward and Forward, built by Harkers of Knottingley in 1954, are shown at the yard as fitting out of these vessels nears completion.

The 9½-mile long Dearne & Dove Canal was built to carry away coal mined in the Barnsley area. This Scrivens view of the canal above Waddingtons' Boatyard at Swinton shows it in the 1920s when it was a through route to Barnsley. There were two more Manvers-size locks just above the boatyard and, despite repeated requests from the owners of Manvers Main Colliery, the S&SYNC refused to enlarge the flight of four locks to Sheffield-size, on the grounds of cost.

Steel and wooden craft worked side by side on the S&SYN from the 1920s until the late 1950s. In any collision between the two types, the latter usually came off second best, leading to leaks and subsequent sinkings. Disposal of redundant wooden vessels by burning was their usual fate and here Waddingtons' Energy is afire in 1960 on the canal bank at Swinton.

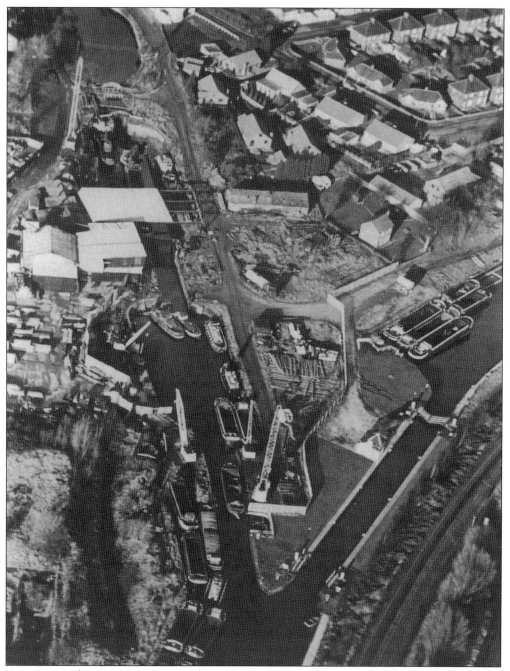

A 1990s aerial view of the area around Waddingtons' Swinton premises, looking north. The Dearne & Dove Canal stretches from top to bottom of the picture as the S&SYN main line bends round to the right. Sheffield-size vessels that were never to be used again, together with tugs and larger barges, litter both the site and the canal below the new 'Waddington Lock'. There are several signs of extension work done at the yard in the 1980s and 1990s, including a covered dock, a widened waterway and the absence of two old Manvers-size locks between the yard and canal junction.

Both the canal and the North Midland Railway's Leeds-Derby line passed beneath the road-carrying Bowbroom Bridge, about a mile up the waterway from the Swinton end after the short Adwick tunnel had been bypassed and the waterway rerouted in the 1830s as the railway was under construction. After a recent talk and slide show devoted to the S&SYN, I was accused of ignoring its most important attraction in failing to mention fishing. Hence these fishermen, featured on a postcard used in 1915 bearing a view looking towards Barnsley. After a steady decline in water quality during the first three-quarters of the twentieth century, fish almost disappeared from the S&SYN. They have now returned thanks to action prompted by increasing environmental awareness.

The Sheffield & South Yorkshire Navigation Co.

DEARNE & DOVE CANAL SUBSIDENCE.

NOTICE IS HEREBY GIVEN that on and from 1st February, 1928, the Company cannot undertake the service of "LIGHT-ENING" Vessels and Boatmen and others concerned, carrying large cargoes, must make their own arrangements for this. Should a flat be available, the Company will loan this at a charge of 10s. per day, payable in advance, until further notice.

By Order.

Navigation Offices,
Exchange Street, Sheffield,
1st Jan. 1928.

The S&SYNC were legally obliged to maintain a draught of 4½ ft on the Dearne & Dove Canal and to keep the waterway in working order. Faced with extensive coal mining subsidence, they found this almost impossible. Initially, they provided flats at their own expense. Cargoes could be lightened into these from a vessel loaded to the guaranteed depth, so that a passage could be effected. In 1927, however, gambling successfully that no one would take up their right to complain to the Lords Commissioners of the Treasury, the company planned to close the canal 'without legal action', initially by issuing this notice. According to the company's minutes of November 1928, this action drove away the captains who had used these flats and also killed off the coal traffic from Mitchells Main to Barnsley Paper Mills. A dam was then placed across the canal above Manvers Main Colliery. Thus the case for closure, which the Minister of Transport was empowered to authorize when a waterway had become disused, was strengthened.

Opened in 1870 and extended over subsequent years, Manvers Main Colliery exported much of its coal by water. When the canal was closed as a through route, it was left open at the Swinton end so that coal could still be collected from Manvers. Until the 1930s the colliery provided free coal for and maintained a lobby equipped with cooking ranges, copper boilers, mangles and scrubbing boards. Here, boatmen's wives could do their baking and laundry during any waiting time. This aerial view shows the bridge from which craft were once loaded direct from tubs brought from the coalface. A vessel is waiting beneath this bridge as another loads at the more modern staithe built to the left of it. The dam and pump installed to maintain the water level below Manvers as the through route was closed are off the left-hand edge of the picture.

Copied from a teapot stand purchased in the 1920s, this view shows a wooden keel facing up the canal moored outside Stanleys' South Yorkshire Soap Works at Wath-on-Dearne.

Between Nos 2 and 3 of the Dearne & Dove Canal's Wombwell flight of locks lay this drawbridge. It carried a railway branch line to collieries at Elsecar and Cortonwood, over what in 1948 was obviously an almost dewatered canal at Brampton. The bridge supports were labelled 'South Yorkshire', indicating the railway company that built it. There was an aqueduct close to the figure on the towpath which carried the waterway over a stream.

The Dearne & Dove's most spectacular feature was undoubtedly the 1,087ft-long Oaks Viaduct with its steel lattice piers. It was opened in 1869 to take the Midland Railway's Barnsley-Cudworth branch line high above the Dearne & Dove and Barnsley Canals, two railways, a main road and the River Dearne. This etching features a view from the Dearne & Dove towpath looking towards Barnsley. (Courtesy of the Alan Hall Collection)

Passenger train services across the viaduct finished in 1958 and the two-coach shuttle service from Cudworth running at about that time is pictured from the canal bank as it approaches Barnsley. The structure was demolished in 1968. (Courtesy of the Alan Hall Collection)

The Dearne & Dove Canal joined the Barnsley Canal above Junction Lock, visible in the background on this postcard view. In front of the house there is a vessel on the Barnsley Canal, which led off left to the River Calder section of the A&CN near Wakefield, crossing a large aqueduct within twenty yards. Behind the cameraman was the route to Barnsley. Both waterways experienced problems with mining subsidence but the S&SYNC seemed to shrug its shoulders, whilst A&CNC workmen attempted to remedy the Barnsley's problem. Consequently, at the lock where the two waterways once met on a level, the Dearne & Dove was always lower than the Barnsley and, according to canal workmen, water was stolen from the latter for many years by wedging open the lock gates.
(Courtesy of the Old Barnsley Collection)

Nine
Swinton to Rotherham

Branfords' Cordale, returning light from Rotherham in 1988 after delivering a cargo of sand for Beatson Clarks, negotiates a path between redundant barges. At that time, these were moored by Waddingtons two abreast on each side of the S&SYN above Swinton Lock. The sand was loaded at East Butterwick on the River Trent at a wharf to which it was delivered by lorry from a quarry at Messingham. Vessels then voyaged to the S&SYN via Goole on a working involving two deliveries a week that lasted for nearly two years. (Courtesy of Andy Horn)

It was the success of Cawoods Hargreaves' venture into push-towing that persuaded BW to build the two tugs mentioned on page 23. The CH tugs worked almost exclusively on the A&CN around Ferrybridge C Power Station, to which they still deliver 510 ton cargoes of coal in three-pan trains. For twelve months in 1993/94, they also loaded at Eastwood, near Rotherham, on the S&SYN. One of the trains loaded there is shown entering Kilnhurst Lock bound for Ferrybridge via the New Junction Canal. This lock was built during the 1979-1983 'improvement' days to replace the original Kilnhurst Flood Lock. For the first few years after the improved S&SYN had been opened, each lock had its own lockkeeper. In the 1990s, however, most of them were replaced by mobile lockkeepers. They used a BW van to travel to and work commercial craft through various stretches of the navigation.

Waddingtons' ex-Furley's motorised keel Rye, heading for Rotherham Mill in September 1968, met a River Don in flood as it left Kilnhurst Cut and was swept backwards. The captain hung a rope onto a workboat moored nearby in a vain attempt to halt his vessel but both craft were then carried towards the weir, though Rye's mate managed to leap ashore. The workboat went over the weir whilst the barge stopped above it. The barge captain was brought ashore by fire services alerted by the mate. Rye's cargo was subsequently grabbed into another barge, Sheaf, using a crane mounted on a BW pontoon, placed between the craft as shown. (Courtesy of Norman Burnitt)

The rail-fed staithe at Roundwood on the left bank of the River Don usually saw queues of keels waiting for over a week to load coal in the 1920s and 1930s. This was the major source of coal for steam trawlers and much of the colliery's output went to Hull. Rafferty & Watson's motor vessel is shown loading at the staithe in 1950. There was a lobby here, as at Manvers Main Staithe, where boatmen's wives could bake and do their laundry during enforced waits. The staithe closed in 1965.

I was aboard the first tow to go down the improved navigation shortly after it had been officially opened in mid 1983. Amazingly, the three-pan tow pushed by the tug Freight Endeavour suddenly stopped dead a few hundred yards below Aldwarke Lock due to insufficient depth of water. The tow is here shown receiving assistance from the former Tom Pudding tug Allerton Bywater which was acting as a workboat nearby. There were more problems on the way to Kilnhurst and further difficulties were encountered at Double Bridges, Mexborough Top Lock and Hexthorpe.

Aldwarke Lock was once a very attractive location on the S&SYN and here, in the 1900s, a loaded wooden keel is seen emerging from the top gates, heading for Rotherham. (Courtesy of the Alan Oliver Collection)

In 1989, Holgates' motor barge John M.Rishworth *and the dumb barge* Florence *were washed over Aldwarke Weir. A huge crane was brought at a crawl for over fifty miles to lift the craft back from whence they came. Here the operation is shown under way.*

At Kilnhurst and Eastwood, the towpath changed sides at junctions between river and canal cut and horses had to be ferried across the waterway. This postcard shows the horse ferry at Eastwood Low Lock, which was pulled across the river on a rope. Horses had not used the service for a couple of decades when it ended in 1962. The cog boat, also shown, was for the lockkeeper's use

Eastwood Lock, the highest up the S&SYN to be built for the 'improved' navigation, is seen here under construction during the early 1980s with the old route visible at an angle ahead. Extensive rerouting of both river and canal were necessary here. Relying on estimates from consultants based in Cloud Cuckoo Land, BW predicted traffic of 'well over two million tons a year at a very conservative estimate' for the completed waterway. The reality has been an average since 1983 of less than one per cent of that figure! (Courtesy of BW)

On 1 June 1983, the improved S&SYN was officially opened during a ceremony at Eastwood Lock. It was planned that several commercial craft would pass through the lock, but a River Don in flood surging past the bottom gates prevented this. Whitakers' Battle Stone, seen entering the lock, stopped here and remained overnight. For aesthetic effect (a loaded vessel seems to look better than a light vessel which rides high in the water) its tanks had been filled with canal water! A large road/rail/canal-served container freight terminal (Rotherport), proposed for construction nearby, never materialised.

The short and private Fitzwilliam/Greasbrough/Parkgate Canal, opened in 1780, left the S&SYN above Eastwood Top Lock, opposite the eventual site of the tram and trolleybus depot on Rawmarsh Road, Rotherham. It served collieries, quarries and ironworks in the Parkgate area, some by means of wagonways. Prior to the coming of the railways, it afforded a lucrative means of exporting coal to Sheffield and other centres of population near the waterways. Two vessels are seen here in the early 1900s, when less than a mile of the canal remained open, moored outside the Basic Slag and Manure Works in Parkgate. There was also a boatyard on the canal, which operated until the waterway closed in the late 1920s.

LAUNCH AT ROTHERHAM.—DREADFUL LOSS OF SIXTY-FOUR LIVES.

This is a copy of the illustration that appeared with a newspaper report of the sinking of the vessel John and William *at Masbrough, near Rotherham. The number of deaths was actually fifty, mainly children who were allowed aboard the vessel as it was launched in 1841. Reportedly, the frenzied axing of holes in the upturned vessel in response to banging from within, 'to allow those trapped to breathe', effectively drowned them as water entered and replaced the pockets of air keeping them alive.*

For the whole period of the S&SYNC's existence, Rotherham Depot was sited below the lock and this photograph, c.1960, looking down the navigation shows several craft moored there. As well as goods to and from Rotherham, Sheffield-bound cargoes were lightened to road transport here, if the vessel carrying them had been loaded to a draught greater than the Sheffield Canal's guaranteed 6ft depth. In 1957, 11,000 tons of cargo were imported through the depot and 151,000 tons of open cast coal, loaded both for Blackburn Meadows Power Station and for delivery to Hull or Goole, were exported. The depot was closed in the late 1960s after Don Street became the head of commercial navigation. (Courtesy of the Graham Hague Collection)

The Sheffield & South Yorkshire Navigation Co.

WARNING

At the Rotherham Borough Police Court on the 3rd December 1936, the Master of a Keel was convicted and fined the sum of Five Pounds for unlawfully aiding and abetting the disposal of Coal in Course of Transit on the Navigation.

**Canal Offices,
Exchange Street, Sheffield, 2.**

The S&SYNC were generous towards their long-serving employees, usually awarding them a pension on retirement and allowing them to live rent-free in the company house that they had occupied during their working life. Like most companies of the time, however, they were ruthless in dealing with dishonesty. Both the bridgekeeper at Tinsley and the Mexborough ferryman were dismissed for withholding tolls. Captains of coal boats often repaid favours from lockkeepers, farmers, friends and boatmen carrying food cargoes, by giving them coal. Both the navigation company and the colliery owners frowned on this practice, often keeping a captain suspected of participating under observation for a few days. They would subsequently take the case to court if they felt that an offence had been committed and then publicise the outcome if he was found guilty. The notice shown here, printed in red ink, was prominently displayed on wharves, locksides and other S&SYNC premises. It relates to the captain of Rupert C who collected a cargo for Hull from Tinsley Park Colliery on the Sheffield Canal's Top Level. The colliery owners claimed in court that as much as 5 tons out of a cargo of 100 tons had at times been found missing when a vessel reached its destination. The captain in this instance had been seen to shovel part of his cargo into a sack. An individual employed at the nearby rolling mills came aboard to 'help him' through Rotherham Lock before leaving with the sack. In his defence, the captain claimed that the sack contained only coal that had fallen onto the deck during loading, which would otherwise have been swept overboard. The value of the coal was stated to be 9d (less than 4p)!

Robinson Brothers took over Rotherham Flour Mill on the River Rother in 1877 and imported their grain by water. During the 1890s and 1900s, they acquired a fleet of four wooden sailing keels (see page 43). One is shown tied up outside their mill in this 1936 newspaper photograph.

When this photograph was taken in 1962, Robinsons' fleet had been sold and ownership of the mill had changed to Ranks. Three Waddington-owned steel motor barges lie moored outside the mill, with Forward beneath the bucket elevator. The silo at the mill had limited capacity and keels were often used as floating storage space to insure against the late arrival of ships and other delays such as ice or floods. Demurrage (compensation for delay) was paid to the keel owner after a wait of four days. Sailing craft had to be winched up the Rother and 'fresh' often made it impossible for a vessel coming downriver to pass beneath Bow Bridge and join the S&SYN main line. (Courtesy of Geoff Warnes)

The mill suffered a serious fire in 1964 and was closed for rebuilding until 1967. The motor barge Mimo, formerly owned by the Goole millers Hudson Wards, is shown discharging at the new silo after its reopening. In those days, twelve cargoes a week were brought there from Hull, giving a 60,000 tons per annum rate. Deliveries by water finished in 1977. This infuriated Victor Waddington who claimed that BW had promised to lengthen the necessary locks out of their annual maintenance budget so that larger craft could be used for the deliveries, thereby making the operation more economic.

The wooden sailing keel Annie Maud, built at Thorne in 1895 for Robinson Brothers, was bought by Waddingtons in 1937 along with the other three members of their fleet. It was immediately motorised before continuing to work to Rotherham mill until displaced by newer steel craft. Annie Maud was then relegated to the internal coal trade until, in the 1970s, it was acquired and restored by York's Castle Mills Museum. It is shown displayed on the River Foss outside the museum in 1978.

Ten
Rotherham to Sheffield

Taken in 1972 before the BACAT traffic began, a bulk cargo is seen being craned out of one of the HS (Humber Small) pans, brought to Rotherham's Don Street Depot by the push tug Freight Pioneer *and transferred to lorry. The depot opened in 1961 and became the head of commercial navigation in 1968. This lasted until 1985 when facilities were moved to Rawmarsh Road (see page 26). It is now a food distribution centre. (Courtesy of BW)*

Founded in 1838, the Holmes Engine & Railway Works built the steam yacht Gazelle, shown here on the canal near their premises in 1860, to demonstrate the advantages of steel plate in shipbuilding. The 57ft-long vessel was exhibited at the Great Exhibition held in London during 1862, travelling down the East Coast under its own steam.

A light, clinker-built wooden keel with a small sail and improvised mast is shown waiting to enter Jordan Lock on this postcard view looking downstream. It dates from the 1910s. A mill goyt goes off to the left. (Courtesy of the Alan Oliver Collection)

Blackburn Meadows Power Station above Jordan Lock began generating in 1921, a second station was opened in 1934 and both were considerably expanded over the next few years. Traffic to the riverside wharf of 100,000 tons of coal a year began in 1939 and lasted until 1965, when it was transferred to rail. This photograph, taken in 1963 looking down the navigation, shows the overhead crane, which was used to discharge cargoes onto a conveyor belt for delivery to the furnaces. During the period of service by water, a 100 ton cargo was unloaded here in the surprisingly short time of twenty minutes. (Courtesy of Graham Hague)

Halfpenny Bridge carrying the towpath between the River Don and the bottom lock of the Sheffield Canal at Tinsley is visible to the left of this postcard view dating from the 1900s. The brick toll-collector's hut on the nearside of the bridge was manned from 5am to 10pm, seven days a week until the outbreak of the Second World War. Foot passengers paid $^1/_2$d to cross and horse marines 1d. After early toll collectors were caught pocketing the takings, the occupant of that post in the 1920s and 1930s was paid only a nominal wage, allowed to keep the tolls and provided with a canal side cottage at a much reduced rent. The bridge was swept away in the floods of 1932 and eventually replaced by the present concrete structure. A clinker-built keel is shown heading down the navigation. After delivering a cargo to Sheffield, many captains bowhauled their vessels down the navigation to collect a load of coal from one of the upper-end collieries, thereby avoiding some towing expenses. For a few years in the 1930s and 1940s, the S&SYNC used tractors to replace horses on the Tinsley flight of locks.

Holiday voyages for youngsters aboard roughly converted former working barges were very popular in the 1970s and 1980s. The *Manvers-size* Charles William *was formerly used by Reckitts to deliver coal from Manvers Main Colliery (when dumb) and, later, Keadby (after being motorised) to their premises at Hull. Here it is shown during that period passing through the third lock up, the Tinsley Flight, on the Sheffield Canal, bound for the city. (Courtesy of Les Reid)*

One of the S&SYN's traditional 15ft x 7ft horse-drawn icebreakers sheathed with galvanised iron is here shown in use in early 1940. It is being rocked from side to side by a team of eight men at Tinsley Turn, three locks up the Sheffield Canal. If the following night produced a keen frost, the canal would become considerably less usable, for the broken ice, as well as preventing lock gates from opening fully, would freeze to the layer that it had been displaced onto. Out of shot to the right lay the pump house, which supplied the canal with most of its water, pumped from the River Don to the top of the Tinsley Flight. Some water for the canal was also provided on the 'Top Level' by Nunnery Colliery.

Nine locks up the Tinsley Flight of twelve locks (reduced to eleven in 1963 as the fifth and sixth locks up were combined to accommodate a new railway bridge) lay House Lock where a canal toll-house was situated. Busy wharves, each with a rail-mounted steam crane, grew up in the pounds between House Lock and the locks above and below (locks three, four and five numbering from the top lock). Sulphur, white sand, moulding sand and other steelworks' cargoes were amongst those discharged here. Craft are here shown in the 1910s moored at the lower wharf as a light vessel, descending the flight, is poled into the fifth lock down. The toll-house was demolished in the 1930s. Its replacement was similarly treated in the early 1960s as the railway to a new marshalling yard was under construction. Two new houses, which still stand, were then built further up the flight. A plaque placed close to the photographer's vantage point informs present day visitors of the enemy bomb which caused damage here in 1940.

In the late 1960s, as Sheffield Basin was again being threatened by redundancy, the Inland Waterways Protection Society organised several 'protest' cruises along the S&SYN between Sheffield and Rotherham. Victor Waddington loaned the society his motor vessel Victory together with Joe Batty, its captain. The vessel is seen heading away from Sheffield carrying society members in Tinsley Top Lock, close to the steelworks that once characterised the East End of the city. This would be the final lock of the voyage for a vessel coming up to Sheffield.

The almost 3 mile long, lock-free part of the Sheffield Canal with eleven bridges between Tinsley Top Lock and Sheffield Basin was usually referred to as the 'Top Level'. A couple of miles away from the basin, at Darnall, the waterway passes over the old Attercliffe to Worksop Turnpike on a stone-built aqueduct. This view shows BW's maintenance narrowboat Naburn passing over it in 1991. In the Second World War, the Government again took over the S&SYN. Just visible beyond Naburn are the remains of one of the seven sets of stop gates placed across the Sheffield Canal at their insistence. These were closed at night and successfully prevented the entire canal from being drained by enemy bombing later that year. The canal was back in full operation within a month.

This 1965 view looks eastwards along the Top Level from Staniforth Road Bridge down Attercliffe Cutting. This was a 150 yard long section dug in 1815 using picks, shovels and wheelbarrows, by hundreds of men unemployed in the recession following the Napoleonic wars. Chapman's survey of 1814 actually entertained the possibility of a tunnel at this point. This was the shallowest stretch of the canal, where powered craft risked picking up car tyres, settees, mattresses, bedsteads and other large items of household refuse on their propellors. The houses shown, on Chippingham Street, have since been demolished and a Supertram Bridge and Cycleway Bridge now cross the waterway between the photographer's position and the distant Shirland Lane Bridge. (Courtesy of Graham Hague)

A photograph taken in the 1950s by Mr R. Frost ten seconds before this one has appeared in several publications entitled 'Through the eye of a needle' because the vessel, Junior T, *appeared unlikely to pass beneath the arch of Bacon Lane Bridge when returning light from Sheffield Basin. According to Jim Shields, the youth seen crouching at the stern of the barge, 'The only problem was if you didn't duck down in time'. Unlike wooden craft, which had to load ballast weights due to limited pumping capacity, steel motor vessels such as this one could readily open a seacock and flood the barge's forepeak, lowering its bow in the water by five inches if necessary. The water would then be removed by the vessel's pumps after clearing the bridges along the top level. It is easy to see the problems that a sailing keel would encounter at bridges such as this if encumbered with its mast and sails on this stage of a voyage.*

This rare but poor quality photograph, published in 1911, was copied from a newspaper. It features the unique craft that Tinsley Park Colliery used from the 1870s to 1928 to transport coal along the Top Level, from their loading staithe on an arm a short distance above Tinsley Top Lock. The coal was brought down from the colliery in wheeled tubs along a narrow gauge rail track and run directly aboard the flat-decked vessel, also fitted with rails. The tubs were loaded fifty to each boat and fastened in four rows as shown. This photograph was taken opposite the colliery company's Effingham Road Depot, below Bernard Road Bridge, where the tubs were wheeled off the vessel. Deliveries were also made to Sheffield Basin. This early example of containerisation had the great advantage of minimising breakage of the coal by eliminating repeated transfer from one medium of transport to another. It was also cheaper, as it required less labour for loading and unloading. In 1911, 92,281 tons of Tinsley Park Colliery's coal was taken away by water, with about half of this delivered to Effingham Road, about a quarter to the basin, and the rest taken to Hull by conventional craft. It is probable that coal coming to Sheffield from the Greasbrough Canal early in the nineteenth century was delivered in a similar manner.

This much-published photograph, taken from the waterway entrance to Sheffield Basin in the 1890s, shows the extent of activity there at the time, with wood, coal and general cargo in evidence. Bills of Lading, brought with cargoes, were handed in to the swing-bridge keeper here, and passed on to the wharf foreman who then relayed details to the barge captain of where he was to moor his vessel. Before nationalisation, tolls charged per mile per ton on the Sheffield Canal were double those charged elsewhere on the S&SYN. Park Goods Siding may be seen to the right and there is an uninterrupted view of the Terminal Warehouse, several years before the Straddle Warehouse (see frontispiece) was built. The extensions to the right hand side of the Terminal Warehouse made by the Manchester, Sheffield & Lincolnshire Railway Company in 1889 can be seen. Most buildings in the basin are now listed structures, as is Bacon Lane Bridge.

A 1965 view of Sheffield Basin taken from a similar angle to the previous photograph. Tomlinson's motor vessel Kitty is arriving with a cargo. In front of a large railway goods warehouse, the timber sheds erected in 1895, 1911 and 1934 can be seen with canopies to shelter four barge berths. An overhead travelling crane was also fitted in 1934. Timber traffic to the basin finished in the mid-1950s and the sheds were subsequently destroyed by fire. (Courtesy of Graham Hague)

The Straddle Warehouse in Sheffield Basin (renamed Victoria Quays as it was being redeveloped in the 1990s) may be seen on the frontispiece of this book to have five arches with four storeys of warehousing above. The two-storey, three-arch image of this unique building stuck onto the funnel of a sea-going vessel, shown in the photograph, stands on a nearby traffic island and serves to demonstrate an artist's failure to do the subject justice.

In 1925 a group of Sheffield millers converted 1889-built extensions to the terminal warehouse in Sheffield Basin into a grain silo. They installed bins, hoppers and a bucket elevator to discharge vessels; thus the millers could receive their wheat in bulk rather than by the sackload. This continued for forty-five years until BW terminated the lease. One of the last vessels to deliver grain from Hull is shown discharging the usual 90-ton cargo at the silo in 1969. Craft brought their loads along the Sheffield Canal on a draught of approximately 6ft. Rotherham and Mexborough mills received 95/100 tons on a $6^{1}/_{2}$ ft draught whilst 110 tons could be brought to Doncaster mill on a 7ft draught. Clarence T delivered the final cargo to the silo, the final cargo into Sheffield Basin, in December 1970. (Courtesy of Graham Hague)